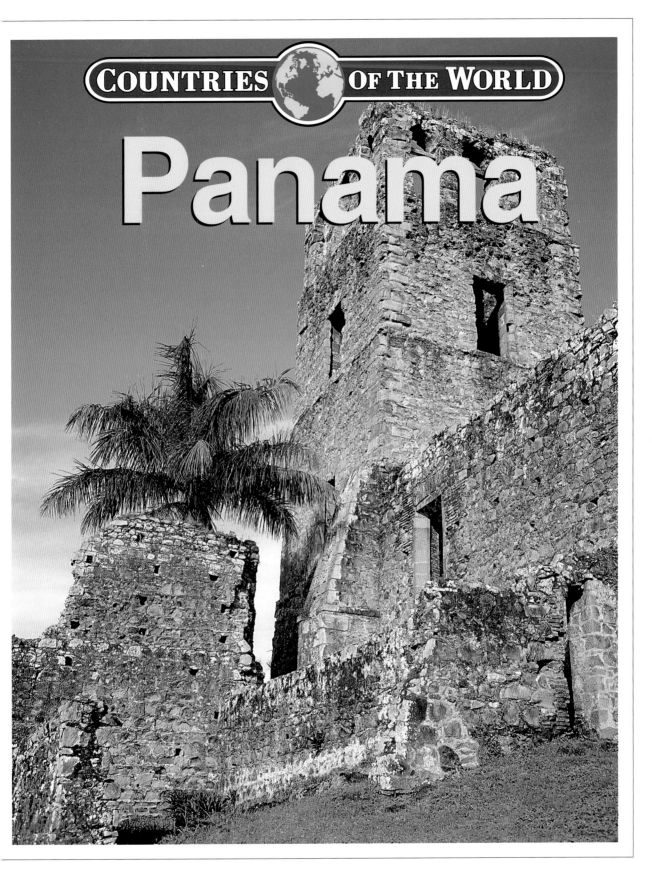

# COUNTRIES OF THE WORLD

# Panama

**Gareth Stevens Publishing**
A WORLD ALMANAC EDUCATION GROUP COMPANY

Written by
**CAROLINA FREIRE**

Edited by
**CHARISSA MARIE NAIR**

Edited in the U.S. by
**ALAN WACHTEL**

Designed by
**BENSON TAN**

Picture research by
**THOMAS KHOO**

First published in North America in 2005 by
**Gareth Stevens Publishing**
A World Almanac Education Group Company
330 West Olive Street, Suite 100
Milwaukee, Wisconsin  53212  USA

Please visit our web site at
**www.garethstevens.com**
For a free color catalog describing
Gareth Stevens Publishing's list of
high-quality books and multimedia programs,
call 1-800-542-2595 (USA) or 1-800-387-3178 (Canada).
Gareth Stevens Publishing's fax: (414) 332-3567.

© **MARSHALL CAVENDISH INTERNATIONAL (ASIA)
PRIVATE LIMITED 2004**
Originated and designed by
Times Editions Marshall Cavendish
An imprint of Marshall Cavendish International (Asia) Pte Ltd
A member of Times Publishing Limited
Times Centre, 1 New Industrial Road
Singapore 536196
http://www.timesone.com.sg/te

**Library of Congress Cataloging-in-Publication Data**
Freire, Carolina.
Panama/ by Carolina Freire.
p. cm. -- (Countries of the world)
Includes bibliographical references and index.
ISBN 0-8368-3117-9 (lib. bdg.)
1. Panama--Juvenile literature.
I. Title. II. Countries of the world (Milwaukee, Wis.)
F1563.2.F74    2004
972.87—dc22                2004041635

Printed in Singapore

1 2 3 4 5 6 7 8 9 08 07 06 05 04

**About the Author:** Panamanian Carolina
Freire earned a bachelor's degree in Foreign
Service from Georgetown University in
Washington, D.C. She went on to earn
a master's degree in public affairs from
the University of Texas, Austin. Freire is
currently living and working in Panama.

**PICTURE CREDITS**
Agence France Presse: 36, 38 (both), 39,
    50 (both), 51, 52, 53, 84
Art Directors & TRIP Photo Library: cover, 3
    (center), 6, 8, 12, 14, 18, 32, 34, 43, 49,
    62, 74, 75, 80
Camera Press: 15 (bottom), 29, 30, 31
Corbis: 13, 16, 47, 69, 82
Corel: 3 (bottom), 56, 57, 73
Focus Team—Italy: 28, 33, 40, 41, 71, 81, 85
Robert Francis/Hutchison Picture Library: 2,
    59, 64
Dr. Jon Fuller/Hutchison Picture Library: 9
    (top), 10 (top), 26, 70
Getty Images/Hulton Archive: 11, 15 (top
    and center), 67, 77, 78
HBL Network Photo Agency: 79
James Davis Travel Photography: 1, 4, 24,
    44, 63
Life File Photo Library: 19
Lonely Planet Images: 5, 9 (bottom), 37, 54,
    55, 60, 61, 72, 83
North Wind Picture Archives: 76
Tan Chung Lee: 42, 45, 91
Topham Picturepoint: 3 (top), 7, 17, 20, 21,
    22, 23, 25, 35, 46, 58, 66, 68
Travel Ink Photo and Feature Library: 10
    (bottom), 27, 48, 65

Digital Scanning by Superskill Graphics Pte Ltd

# Contents

# AN OVERVIEW OF PANAMA

Strategically positioned between the North and South American continents and also between the Atlantic and Pacific oceans, the Republic of Panama can be described as being at the crossroads not only of the Americas but also of the world.

Panama was a Spanish colony for three centuries before declaring its independence from Spain in 1821. For much of the nineteenth century, however, Panama was part of Colombia, from which Panama declared its independence in 1903.

For a relatively small country, Panama is home to numerous national parks and nature reserves, all of which help to support the country's remarkably diverse collection of plants and animals. Panamanians are a warm and sociable people.

*Opposite:* **Completed in 1962, the Bridge of the Americas links not only the two halves of the Panamanian isthmus but also the North and South American continents. For nearly thirty years, the Panama Canal divided the isthmus.**

*Below:* **Panamanian children from a remote village in the province of Bocas del Toro play near a water pump.**

## THE FLAG OF PANAMA

The Panamanian flag is divided into four equally sized rectangles. The top-left and bottom-right quarters are white. The top-right rectangle is red, and the bottom-left rectangle is blue. A five-pointed star is positioned in the middle of each of the white rectangles. The top star is blue, while the bottom star is red. The colors red and blue respectively represent the Liberal and Conservative parties, the two main political parties at the time of Panama's independence. White symbolizes peace between the two parties. Designed by Manuel E. Amador Jr., the son of Panama's first president, Manuel Amador Guerrero (1883–1909), the flag was adopted in 1904.

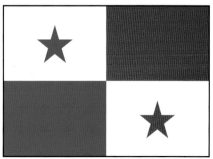

# Geography

## A Strategic Location

Connecting North and South America is an isthmus, or narrow strip of land that joins two pieces of land. Panama occupies the easternmost section of this isthmus and has a land area of about 29,332 square miles (75,990 square kilometers). The country's total area, which includes the Gulf of Panama, is about 30,185 square miles (78,200 square km). The Panama Canal roughly divides the isthmus into eastern and western halves.

Panama is bordered by the Caribbean Sea to the north, the Pacific Ocean to the south, Colombia to the east, and Costa Rica to the west. Located off the southern border of eastern Panama, the Gulf of Panama is an inlet of the Pacific Ocean. The Caribbean Sea is an extension of the Atlantic Ocean.

## The Gulf of Panama

Measuring 115 miles (185 km) from east to west at its widest point and about 100 miles (160 km) from north to south, the Gulf of Panama is divided into northern, western, and eastern sections.

**OFFSHORE ISLANDS**

Apart from those within the parameters of the Gulf of Panama, many nearby islands are also part of Panamanian territory. Parida Island, Coiba Island, and Cébaco Island are found off the country's Pacific coast, while the Bocas del Toro Archipelago and the San Blas Islands are located off its Caribbean coast.

*Below:* Forming part of Panama's Pacific coastline, Coronado Beach is situated about 50 miles (80 km) west of Panama City, the country's capital city.

The western section is known as Gulf of Parita, while the eastern section is known as the Gulf of San Miguel. The Bay of Panama forms the gulf's north. A number of islands, including Contadora Island and the Pearl Islands, dot the waters in between the Bay of Panama and the Gulf of San Miguel.

## Many Mountain Ranges

Panama is marked by a series of mountain ranges. The Tabasará Mountains dominate the western half of Panama, and the Talamanca Range, which straddles southeastern Costa Rica and northwestern Panama, contains Mount Fábrega, the country's second-highest point, at 10,939 feet (3,334 meters). Also known as the Volcán de Chiriquí, Barú Volcano is located in between the Tabasará Mountains and the Talamanca Range. Panama's highest peak, Barú Volcano measures about 11,400 feet (3,475 m) high. Mount Santiago, which marks the western end of the Tabasará Mountains, is the country's third-highest peak, at 9,269 feet (2,825 m). In the eastern half of Panama, the Cordillera de San Blas and the Darién Mountains form parts of the country's northern frontier, while the Sapo and Majé Mountains define stretches of its southern border.

*Above:* In 1998, Panama experienced a severe drought that led to a drop in the water level of the Chagres River. The Chagres and Tuira Rivers are two of Panama's more important rivers. The country also has many short rivers that flow perpendicular to its coasts.

# A Tropical Maritime Climate

Panama is generally hot and humid and has been described as having a tropical maritime climate. Temperatures in Panama's coolest months seldom fall below 79° F (26° C). Although the country is said to have two seasons — dry and rainy — the weather conditions of these seasons vary from region to region. Regions on the northern side of the Tabasará Mountains, for example, receive significantly more rain than those to the south. Because of yearly rain-bearing trade winds, Panama's northern Caribbean coast receives as much as 50 inches (1,270 millimeters) more rain than the southern Pacific coast. The Chiriquí region in Panama's southwest has a dry season that is more distinctly felt than elsewhere in the country. The dry season in Chiriquí lasts from January to April, and March is the region's driest month. Unlike western Panama, both coastal regions of eastern Panama that approach the Colombian border receive ample rainfall throughout the year.

Panama can be divided into three climatic zones — hot, temperate, and cold. Nearly 90 percent of the country's land is below 2,300 feet (701 m) in altitude; this is the low, hot zone. Regions between 2,300 and about 4,900 feet (701 and 1,494 m) form the temperate zone, which accounts for most of the remaining 10 percent. The cold zone consists of the few areas in Panama above 4,900 feet (1,494 m) in altitude.

**THE DARIÉN JUNGLE**

Some estimate that 70 percent of the world's land-dwelling creatures can be found in tropical forests. The United Nations Educational, Scientific, and Cultural Organization (UNESCO) has, to date, named forty-eight areas of tropical forest as World Heritage sites. The Darién jungle is among them.
*(A Closer Look, page 54)*

**NATIONAL PARKS AND WONDERS**

For a relatively small country, Panama has many protected natural environments. These areas amount to a total of about 17 percent of the country's area.
*(A Closer Look, page 60)*

*Left:* **Plentiful rainfall helps Panama's dense tropical forests stay moist and green. Humidity levels are about 80 percent but can climb to higher levels in the forests, especially during the rainy season.**

*Left:* **The unusual Peanut-head bug (*Fulgora laternaria*) belongs to the Fulgorid family of insects and can be spotted in Panama's rain forests. Most Peanut-head bugs measure about 3 inches (8 cm) long.**

## MANATEES: A DYING BREED

**A modest number of West Indian manatees (*Trichechus manatus*) live in Panama's waters.**

(*A Closer Look, page 56*)

## SAVING THE HARPY EAGLE

**The Harpy eagle (*Harpia harpyja*) is the national bird of Panama and also an endangered species.**

(*A Closer Look, page 72*)

*Below:* **Wild populations of the Strawberry Poison Dart frog (*Dendrobates pumilio*) can only be found in Nicaragua, Costa Rica, and Panama. These frogs grow to an average length of about 1.25 inches (3 cm).**

# Plant and Animal Life

Plant life in Panama is diverse and is found in areas ranging from tropical rain forests to savannas to montane forests. In keeping with the country's rainfall patterns, tropical rain forests dominate Panama's well-watered, northern regions, while savannas are common in the country's drier, southwestern regions. The forests in Panama's northern regions are home to deciduous trees, including the wild cashew and the rubber tree. The country also has over a thousand species of orchids, which are found at low and high altitudes. In Panama's temperate, highland regions, montane forests and cultivated crops, such as coffee, grow.

Because of its geographical location, Panama's rich animal life consists of species that migrated from North into South America or vice versa. Jaguars, tapirs, and deer are some of the originally North American species that inhabit Panama, while the country's sloths, anteaters, and armadillos are members of species that originated in South America. Flanked by two oceans, Panama's marine life is extensive and includes beautiful and complex coral reefs and giant sea turtles that lay their eggs on the country's beaches. The country boasts nearly 950 species of birds — a remarkable number for a relatively small country.

# History

## The Native Peoples of Panama

Stone tools that have been unearthed in present-day Panama suggest that the isthmus was inhabited as early as 10,000 B.C. The region's early peoples not only hunted, fished, and gathered edible vegetation for food, but also cultivated crops. Archaeological evidence suggests that corn and other root vegetables were cultivated in Panama from as early as between 7000 and 5000 B.C. Over thousands of years, the early peoples of Panama developed into the Amerindian, or American Indian, groups in the country today, such as the Chocó and Kuna.

In about 2800 B.C., central Panama was already home to some of the earliest pottery-making centers in the Americas. The Monagrillo culture had methods of production that, although crude, were used for many centuries. Amerindian craftsmanship, society, and culture grew more and more sophisticated over time with older settlements becoming regional centers and new villages arising. By the years between A.D. 300 and A.D. 450, Amerindian civilization and cultural life had reached remarkable heights. By A.D. 500, Panama's Amerindians had established the tradition of making ceramics decorated in yellows and reds. The artifacts of that era also included ornaments made from gold or carved shells and bones, and stone sculptures of human figures.

*Above:* An example of the sophisticated pre-Colombian pottery produced in Panama, this vessel has three hollow legs, each with a ball that rolls up and down inside it.

*Left:* Several prehistoric drawings have been etched into the surface of this large rock near the city of Boquete, in the province of Chiriquí. Many believe these drawings were made by the Amerindians hundreds of years ago.

*Left:* **Vasco Núñez de Balboa** (*center*) **points while his crew marvels at the Pacific Ocean, which Balboa claimed for Spain.**

## SIXTEENTH-CENTURY AMERINDIANS

By the time the Spanish arrived in 1501, the isthmus was dominated by Chocó and Chibcha Amerindians. Gold mining and craft-making had been part of the economies and cultures of these groups for about 1,000 years.

# The First Spaniards

In 1501, Spaniards Rodrigo de Bastidas, Juan de la Cosa, and Vasco Núñez de Balboa became the first Europeans to reach the isthmus. They had sailed west from present-day Venezuela, which Italian explorer Christopher Columbus had claimed for Spain in 1498. Early attempts by the Spanish to establish settlements on parts of the isthmus drew much resistance from the native Amerindians and spurred Balboa, in particular, to adopt some heavy-handed measures against the natives. Balboa then established Santa María de la Antigua del Darién, the first permanent settlement on the isthmus, and assumed leadership of the colony. In 1513, Balboa and his men completed a trek from the Atlantic to the Pacific coast of the isthmus. He claimed the Pacific Ocean for Spain and returned to Santa María in January 1514. In 1519, Pedro Arias de Ávila, the newly appointed and reputedly ruthless governor, ordered Balboa's execution because he saw Balboa as a threat to his power. That same year, the people of Santa María moved to a new town called Panama.

## PANAMA CITY

The capital city of Panama has a history that dates back to the early sixteenth century. Before the Spanish arrived, Panamá, which means "many fish," was an Amerindian fishing village.

*(A Closer Look, page 64)*

# Spanish Colonization

In the course of nearly 300 years, from the early 1500s to the early 1800s, Panama came to serve Spain not only as a strategic and profitable trade center, but also as a starting point for the conquest of Peru.

In 1538, Spain granted Panama the status of *audiencia* (aw-dee-EN-see-ah), which gave it some degree of autonomy. As Panama prospered, Nombre de Dios, a settlement that was founded in 1510 but had since faded in importance, revived. Roads were created between Nombre de Dios and Panama, and Nombre de Dios gained a reputation for the impressive *ferias* (FEH-ree-ahs), or trade fairs, that were organized there.

In the late 1500s, Englishman Francis Drake led a crippling attack on Nombre de Dios. Portobelo then became the new center for trade and ferias. Commerce in the area peaked in the early 1600s. In 1671, however, Welshman Henry Morgan and his crew plundered and destroyed the town of Panama. Portobelo was razed to the ground in 1739. That same year, Panama ceased to be an audiencia and was placed under the viceroyalty of New Granada, which also included much of the northern part of South America. Despite the rebuilding of the towns of Panama (1673) and Portobelo (1751), civilization on the isthmus had entered a period of decline.

## THE ROYAL ROAD

In the early years of Spanish colonization, amassing gold, silver, and pearls was the main goal of the Spaniards who came to the New World.

To transport their valuable goods back to Europe, the Spaniards would sail from other Spanish-controlled areas in South America to Panama's southern coast. There, the goods would be transferred to Europe-bound ships docked along the Atlantic coast of the isthmus.

This inland route was known to some as Camino Real, or the Royal Road. More famously, however, it was also known as the Camino de Cruces, or the Road of the Crosses, because of the many people who had died on the route and were buried there.

*Left:* **Forts built by the Spanish in the seventeenth and eighteenth centuries to protect their treasure-laden ships still stand in Portobelo today. In 1980, UNESCO declared Portobelo a World Heritage Site.**

*Left:* **A large ship passes through the Gatún Locks of the Panama Canal on its way to the Pacific Ocean. The Gatún Locks control the northern third of the Panama Canal.**

# The Struggle for Independence

In the early 1800s, calls for autonomy echoed throughout Spanish America. Panama, however, did not join the independence movement until some Spanish merchants suceeded in legally barring the people of the isthmus from engaging in trade with non-Spanish foreigners. In 1821, Panama seceded from Spain and joined Gran Colombia, a union of present-day Colombia, Venezuela, and Ecuador. Up until 1843, when a new constitution for Gran Colombia was passed, Panamanians were free to elect their own governor. Not long after the new constitution came into effect, Panama was reduced to being a state of Colombia and was unable to break free until the beginning of the twentieth century.

On November 3, 1903, a Panamanian revolutionary junta, with the support of the United States, defied Colombian authority and declared Panama's independence. The Colombian government tried to quash the rebellion, but its attempts to send troops into Panama were thwarted by U.S. intervention. Manuel Amador Guerrero became Panama's first president in 1904. That same year, the United States secured from Panamanian authorities the rights to use, occupy, and control the Canal Zone, the 10-mile (16 km)-wide area that was to be divided by the Panama Canal. The Panama Canal opened on August 15, 1914.

## THE PANAMA RAILROAD

In 1847, the government of Gran Colombia awarded the project of building a transcontinental railroad through Panama to U.S. investors. After a number of setbacks, which delayed its opening, the railroad became fully operational in 1855.
*(A Closer Look, page 66)*

## THE PANAMA CANAL

Responding to growing U.S. interest in creating a passage between the Atlantic and Pacific oceans, President Theodore Roosevelt supported approaching the Colombian government for the rights to build a canal through Panama in 1902. The Colombian government rejected the proposal in 1903.
*(A Closer Look, page 62)*

*Left:* General Manuel Antonio Noriega Morena (*front, far right*) ruled Panama with an iron fist in the 1980s.

# From Dictatorships to Democracy

Colonel Omar Torrijos Herrera slowly gained control of the military junta that had forcibly taken control of the country in 1968. Despite his dictatorship, Torrijos did not become unpopular. His decision to beautify Panama City through public construction, which caused the country to run up heavy debts, won the hearts of many Panamanians. His successful negotiation of a treaty in the late 1970s that forced the United States to turn over control of the Panama Canal to Panama by the end of 1999 also made him popular.

Torrijos died in 1981, and two years later, Colonel Manuel Antonio Noriega Morena, another dictator, seized the country. Panama swiftly descended into chaos under Noriega, whose regime was not only harsh, but also corrupt. The regime rigged the results of the 1984 presidential election, Noriega's political opponents were murdered, and by early 1987, Noriega had become the subject of a drug-trafficking scandal. In response, the United States imposed tough trade sanctions on Panama in 1988. In December 1989, growing conflict between Panamanian and U.S. military personnel sparked a military invasion by the United States that led to the restoration of democracy in Panama. Since the invasion, the Panamanian government has been heavily reformed so that it upholds democratic principles and institutions that prevent the country from becoming a dictatorship again.

## THE BRIDGE OF THE AMERICAS

Completed in 1962, the Bridge of the Americas is widely regarded as the second-most important engineering project in the country, after the Panama Canal.
*(A Closer Look, page 48)*

## BEFORE THE DICTATORSHIPS

For sixty-five years (1903–1968), Panama officially maintained a constitutional democracy, but the country actually was controlled by a few powerful men. In the late 1940s and 1950s, the Panamanian police became increasingly involved in the country's politics, leading to the establishment of a military junta in 1968.

# Vasco Núñez de Balboa (1475–1519)

Although Spanish explorer Vasco Núñez de Balboa was not officially the first European to set foot on the isthmus, he made history by becoming the first European to see the Pacific Ocean from the isthmus. On September 5, 1513, Balboa and a crew of 190 Spaniards and 1,000 Amerindians began a punishing 45-mile (72-km) trek through the thick forests that separated the isthmus's Caribbean and Pacific coasts. The group's journey ended twenty-four days later. Upon returning to the colony of Darién, which he helped found, Balboa and Darién's new governor had a disagreement. Balboa was later accused of an offense he did not commit and beheaded in his homeland in 1519.

**Vasco Núñez de Balboa**

# Ferdinand de Lesseps (1805–1894)

Former French diplomat Ferdinand de Lesseps was the man behind the construction of the Suez Canal, a passage between the Red and the Mediterranean Seas. The Suez Canal took ten years to complete (1859–1869) and was a success. In 1879, the International Congress of Geographical Sciences approved the construction of the Panama Canal and appointed de Lesseps to lead the project. De Lesseps was unsuccessful in Panama, however, because harsh terrain made the engineering demands of the Panama Canal more challenging than those of the Suez Canal. The uncomfortable climate and tropical diseases also made de Lesseps's task harder. The Panama Canal finally was finished after U.S. efforts continued where de Lesseps left off. De Lesseps did not live to see the opening of the Panama Canal.

**Ferdinand de Lesseps**

# Mireya Elisa Moscoso (1946– )

In 1999, Mireya Elisa Moscoso de Gruber became the first woman in Panamanian history to be elected president. She is the widow of former Panamanian president Arnulfo Arias Madrid, who died in 1988. Arias was the popularly elected president whom Colonel Omar Torrijos overthrew in 1968. In 1990, Moscoso helped establish the Arnulfista Party. She became the party's leader the following year. Moscoso first ran for the presidency in 1994, coming in second with 29 percent of the vote. In the 1999 elections, Martin Torrijos, the son of Omar Torrijos, was Moscoso's main opponent.

**Mireya Moscoso**

# Government and the Economy

## A Constitutional Democracy

Panama's government is a constitutional democracy that is made up of three main branches — executive, legislative, and judicial. The executive branch is led by the president and two vice-presidents. All three leaders are popularly elected to serve five-year terms, and none are eligible for reelection. President Mireya Elisa Moscoso, First Vice President Arturo Ulises Vallarino, and Second Vice President Dominador "Kaiser" Baldonero Bazan were elected in 1999. The president appoints the cabinet of ministers.

The legislative branch consists of a unicameral, or one-house, parliament called the Asamblea Legislativa, or Legislative Assembly. The Legislative Assembly is made up of seventy-two members, and each member is elected by popular vote to serve a five-year term. Members of the Legislative Assembly are eligible for reelection. The most recent elections were held in May 2004.

*Below:* **Located in Panama City, the Panama National Assembly Building is where members of the country's Asamblea Legislativa, or Legislative Assembly, gather to make laws.**

The judicial branch is dominated by the Corte Suprema de Justicia, or the Supreme Court of Justice, which is the highest court in the land. Nine judges serve on the country's Supreme Court, each of whom was appointed by the president and approved by the Legislative Assembly to serve a ten-year term. Within the Supreme Court are different divisions that deal with civil, penal, and administrative cases. Below the Supreme Court is a system of lower courts, including five superior courts and three courts of appeal.

## Local Government

Panama is divided into thirteen administrative regions — nine provinces and four *comarcas* (kow-MAHR-kahz), or special territories for indigenous groups. The comarcas and their groups are Kuna Yala (San Blas), Emberá (Emberá-Wounaan), Madungandí (Madungandí), and Ngobe Buglé (Guaymí). The provinces are Bocas del Toro, Chiriquí, Coclé, Colón, Darién, Herrera, Los Santos, Panamá, and Veraguas, and they are further divided into sixty-five municipal districts. Every province is led by a governor, and each comarca is led by a tribal leader.

**SECURITY FORCES**

Panama officially does not have a military. In 1990, the government abolished Panama's armed forces and replaced them with several security forces, one of which is the presidential guards (*above*). In 1994, the Panamanian parliament passed a constitutional amendment preventing the formation of a full-fledged military. Today, Panama's security forces consist of the Panamanian Public Forces (PPF), which include the Panamanian National Police, National Maritime Service, and National Air Service.

17

# Economy

Panama's geographical location has greatly influenced its economic development. Since colonial times, the country has been viewed as a strategic point for trade and transit, a role that was reinforced with the opening of the Panama Canal in 1914. Control of the Panama Canal was placed in the hands of local authorities in December 1999. Now businesses located along the canal dominate Panama's service industry. The Panama Canal is the single largest employer in the country. Banking and tourism are also important contributors of income generated by Panama's service sector. From 2000 to 2002, Panama's economy was hindered by the withdrawal of U.S. military personnel from the country.

# Division of Labor

At the beginning of the twenty-first century, the Panamanian work force consisted of more than one million people. Unskilled workers, however, far outnumbered skilled workers, and in 2002, 16 percent of the Panamanian work force was unemployed. The most recent available figures suggest that just over 61 percent of

## AGRICULTURE AND INDUSTRY

Panama's industrial and agricultural sectors lag quite far behind the country's service sector. Panama's modest industrial sector produces cement and other construction materials, petroleum products, clothing, and refined sugar. Panama's farmers grow mainly bananas, rice, corn, coffee, sugarcane, and vegetables for both domestic consumption and export. Fishing also provides income through frozen seafood exports.

## MARITIME SERVICES

Combining Panama's strategic geographical location and the opening of the Panama Canal gave the country unparalleled advantage in the maritime industry. After Panama gained control of the Panama Canal in 1999, providing world-class maritime services became one of the nation's main industries and income earners.
*(A Closer Look, page 58)*

*Left:* **A group of Panamanian men unloads boxes of bananas from a truck.**

working-age Panamanians are employed in the service sector. About 21 percent of the Panamanian work force is employed in agriculture, while 18 percent work in the industrial sector. In 2001, the service sector provided 76 percent of the country's gross domestic product (GDP). Industry and agriculture accounted for the remaining 24 percent of the GDP, at 17 and 7 percent, respectively. In 1999, it was estimated that 37 percent of Panamanians lived below the poverty line.

*Above:* **The Banco Nacional de Panamá, or the National Bank of Panama, is the country's central bank. It provides services such as currency exchanges. Banco Nacional de Panamá is located in Panama City.**

## Trade Partners

The United States is Panama's largest trade partner. In 2001, Panama sold nearly half of its exports to the United States. Other countries, including Nicaragua, Sweden, and Costa Rica, imported Panamanian goods in far smaller quantities. Agricultural products, such as bananas, shrimp, sugar, and coffee, dominate Panamanian exports.

Panama imports crude oil, foodstuffs, consumer goods, and chemicals from other countries to meet the country's domestic needs. Panama buys about one-third of its imported goods from the United States. Apart from the United States, Panama also buys goods from Ecuador, Venezuela, and Japan.

# People and Lifestyle

## A People of Mixed Heritage

In 2004, over 3 million people were estimated to be living in Panama. Most Panamanians, 63.3 percent of the country's population, are between the ages of fifteen and sixty-four, while 30.6 percent are age fourteen and younger. Panamanians age sixty-five and older form 6.1 percent of the country's population. The Panamanian population is more or less equally divided between men and women, although women tend to outlive men. In Panama, men live for an average of about seventy years, while women live for nearly seventy-five years.

The vast majority of Panamanians are of mixed heritage. Mestizos, or people of mixed Amerindian and Caucasian heritage, form about 70 percent of the country's population, while people of West Indian, or mixed Amerindian and African, descent form about 14 percent. Ten percent of Panamanians are Caucasian, and the remaining 6 percent are Amerindian. Arabs and Chinese make up small minorities in Panama.

**AMERINDIANS IN PANAMA**

The Chocó, Guaymí, and Kuna are Panama's three main Amerindian groups. The Emberá and Wounaan belong to the larger Chocó group of peoples. The Chocó, Guaymí, and Kuna continue to uphold traditional lifestyles in the twenty-first century.
(*A Closer Look, page 44*)

*Below:* The Panamanians living in this settlement are of West Indian heritage.

## Urban and Rural Settlement Patterns

Most urban Panamanians live in cities on either side of the Panama Canal. The country's capital city, Panama City; San Miguelito; Colón; La Chorrera; and Cristóbal are some such cities. The Chagres River flows through the urban areas surrounding the Panama Canal, so they are sometimes collectively called the Chagres region. Panama City is not only the country's capital and largest urban center but also the industrial, commercial, political, and cultural hub of the nation. San Miguelito, which has a population that is 70 percent that of Panama City's, is the country's second-largest city.

Most rural Panamanians live in the wide area between the Azuero Peninsula and the Tabasará Mountains. The terrain in this region is characterized by plains and low hills. The extremely mountainous east of Panama, particularly the large province of Darién, is inhospitable and is the country's least populated region. The areas north of the Tabasará Mountains also have few people.

*Above:* Founded in 1850 by Americans who were working on the Panama Railroad, Colón was once a prosperous city. Today, however, much of Colón is taken up by slums, as more and more of the city's people struggle against poverty. In 1953, the city established the Colón Free Trade Zone, which continues to be the world's second-largest duty-free port.

# Public Health

Health care in Panama can be sought at either public or private institutions, although treatment at private facilities can be too expensive for many Panamanians. Panama's social security administration, together with the country's Ministry of Health, supports and monitors the country's health institutions, which include hospitals, hospital clinics, regional health centers, and mobile medical units. Under the country's social security system, most Panamanians who are employed full-time are entitled to free or subsidized health care at state-funded institutions. Most Panamanian cities have some form of heath-care facility. Some estimates suggest that there are 562 Panamanians for every doctor in the country.

# Health in Rural Areas

Monitoring and improving public health in rural Panama, however, has been an uphill climb for both the government and local health-care professionals. In the country's rural regions, the most important health-related needs include basic sanitation facilities and the availability of clean drinking water. Toward

*Below:* **In the early 1980s, improving basic sanitation standards and increasing the availability of clean drinking water were high priorities not only in rural Panama but also in the country's urban slums.**

the end of the twentieth century, many sanitation and water treatment facilities in rural Panama were overused and in need of repair. Cuts in government spending, however, have prevented improvements and repairs from taking place.

*Above:* **Homeless and jobless Panamanians, including this man, who has been living in abandoned train carriages for years, are not entitled to free health care at the country's public clinics.**

## HIV/AIDS in Panama

HIV stands for "human immunodeficiency virus," which is the virus that causes AIDS. AIDS stands for "acquired immunodeficiency syndrome." AIDS is a gradual weakening of the body's immune system — the body's natural defense mechanism — that eventually leads to death.

In 2001, Panama had a population of about 25,000 people living with HIV/AIDS. About 1,900 Panamanian HIV/AIDS sufferers died that year. Today, Panamanian health authorities are working closely with international aid agencies in an attempt to reduce the negative effects of the disease on Panamanian society through funding, medical assistance, and community education. In October 2003, Panama held a conference to explore the most recent discoveries made in the field of treating people with HIV/AIDS.

# Education

In 2003, Panama had a literacy rate of more than 92 percent. Slightly more male Panamanians age fifteen and older are able to read and write than females of the same age.

The Panamanian education system consists of three main stages — primary, secondary, and higher education. Education is compulsory and free for Panamanians between the ages of six and fifteen, and Spanish is the language of instruction. Panama's Ministerio de Educación, or Ministry of Education, oversees the country's primary and secondary schools.

In Panama, primary, or elementary, school lasts for six years, while secondary, or high, school is split into two three-year stages: general and academic. Upon completing general secondary school, students have the option of pursuing academic secondary education, which also lasts for three years. Education at the academic stage is more specialized and prepares students for higher education. Students who graduate from academic secondary school receive a Bachillerato de Ciencias, de Letras, or de Comercio, each of which is equivalent to a high school diploma.

*Opposite:* **Student activists from the Universidad de Panamá (University of Panama) waited for law enforcement officers to arrive after they blocked off the Transisthmian Highway just outside the university in 2000. The students were protesting against the Panamanian government's decision to allow the United States to set up an antidrug center near the canal because they believed that the center was just an excuse for the United States to maintain a military presence in Panama.**

*Below:* **These Kuna Amerindian children are attending primary school.**

# Higher Education

Panamanians can pursue higher education at both university and nonuniversity levels. At universities, Panamanian students can choose from a wide variety of fields, including architecture, agriculture, law, medicine, and marine engineering. Nonuniversity higher-education institutions include teacher training colleges and vocational institutes. At the latter, students acquire specialized skills in specific trades. Graduates of teacher training colleges teach in either primary or secondary schools.

The Council of Rectors of Public and Private Universities oversees and monitors the development of higher education in Panama. Public universities in Panama include Universidad Tecnológica de Panamá (Technological University of Panama) and Universidad Latinoamericana de Ciencia y Tecnologia, Panamá (Scientific and Technological Latin American University). Universidad Santa María la Antigua (University of Santa María la Antigua) is a private Roman Catholic institution.

**PANAMA'S OLDEST UNIVERSITY**

Founded in 1935, Universidad de Panamá (University of Panama) is the largest and the oldest institution of higher education operating in the country. The university began as the National Institute In Panama City. Panama's first university, however, was a Jesuit university established in the mid-eighteenth century. Because of religious and political conflicts, the university closed its doors after less than twenty years.

# Religion

The Panamanian constitution promises freedom of religion, and there is no state religion. The vast majority of Panamanians, however, are Christian. About 85 percent of Panamanians are Roman Catholics, while Protestant Panamanians have been estimated to make up between 5 and 15 percent of the population. Minority religions in the country include Islam, Judaism, and Hinduism. Jewish and Muslim Panamanians form the largest minority religious groups. Religion does not have a history of causing social conflict in Panama.

## Christianity

Roman Catholic Panamanians practice their religion to varying degrees. Some try to incorporate as much of the religion into their lives as they can and make it a point to attend church services every day, while others, especially those living in urban centers, tend to be less observant of religious customs. Most Roman Catholic Panamanians, however, usually observe religious

*Left:* The Catedral Metropolitan (Metropolitan Cathedral) took over a century to build and is a fine example of Spanish colonial architecture. This Roman Catholic cathedral is located in a historic district of Panama City.

*Left:* **The Elmslie Memorial United Church is a Presbyterian institution. Presbyterians, as well as other nonevangelical Protestant denominations, are concentrated in the provinces of Panamá and Colón.**

holidays, such as Good Friday, Easter, and Christmas, and honor rites of passage, such as baptism and confirmation ceremonies. In Panama, women are expected and tend to be more religious than men. Archbishop Jose Dimas Cedeno Delgado is the highest-ranking Roman Catholic religious leader in Panama.

Numerous Protestant denominations are present in Panama. The Mormons, Seventh-Day Adventists, Jehovah's Witnesses, and Episcopalians are some of these groups. Protestant churches have been growing, partly because some Roman Catholics have left the Roman Catholic Church to join Protestant churches.

## Islam in Panama

Islam is believed to have arrived in Panama in the mid-sixteenth century. Panama's first Muslims were Africans whom the Spanish had captured to work as slaves on the isthmus. Because of widespread discrimination and persecution, the number of Muslims gradually declined until the late nineteenth and early twentieth centuries. By that time, the Muslims in Panamanian territory were mostly merchants from South Asia or the Middle East. Construction on the first mosque in Panama City began in the mid-twentieth century. West Indians, or people of mixed Amerindian and African descent, from nearby countries, such as Jamaica, Trinidad, and Barbados, made up most of the new converts to Islam in Panama.

### SUNNI AND SHI'ITE MUSLIMS

**Muslims of the world are divided into two main groups — Sunnis and Shi'ites. Although the two groups are separated by some differences in religious doctrines, followers of both groups share many practices, such as abstaining from pork and alcohol and fasting from dawn to dusk during the Islamic holy month of Ramadan. For both groups, the Qu'ran is the Islamic holy book. Muslim Panamanians today are mostly Sunnis.**

# Language and Literature

## Spanish, English, and Other Languages

Although Spanish is Panama's official language, many Panamanians are bilingual. Up to 14 percent of the population is proficient in English. Spanish is, nevertheless, the language used in government, trade, and education. Most Panamanians who speak English use the language only in business settings. Some Panamanians speak a type of pidgin English some language experts have named "Southwestern Caribbean Creole English." Pidgin English incorporates influences from the native languages of a land and is not always understood by native English speakers.

Apart from Spanish and English, Panamanians are also known to speak nine Amerindian languages, including Buglere, Teribe, Kuna, Emberá, Woun Meu (the language of the Wounaan), and Ngäbere (the language of the Guayamí). The country's larger racial minorities, including the Chinese and Arabs, often speak the languages of their ethnic cultures. While the Arabs speak Arabic, Panama's Chinese speak mostly either Hakka or Cantonese.

*Left:* A Panamanian woman reads a local Spanish-language newspaper. Panamanian newspapers do not always enjoy freedom of the press. Until President Moscoso came to power in 1999, strict laws prevented Panama's media from scrutinizing and commenting on prominent figures in Panamanian society. President Moscoso has since abolished some of these laws to create a freer press, but tight restrictions on the media still exist in Panama.

# Panamanian Literature

Distinctively Panamanian literature began to emerge only in the twentieth century. Its development has been relatively modest. As a result, Panamanian literature is rarely identified independently from Latin American literature. Latin American literature includes works from Spanish-speaking countries throughout the Americas.

Historically, literary works circulating in Panama were usually by Mexican, Peruvian, and Colombian authors, a tradition still deeply rooted in Panamanian reading habits today. Ricardo Miró (1883–1940) is probably the most revered of Panamanian authors and poets. Miró published his first book in 1908. His noted works include *The Legend of the Pacific* (1919) and *Ways* (1929). He is said to have led Panamanian poetry into a new era. Today, a literary prize is named in his honor and is awarded to Panamanian writers of exceptional talent. Contemporary Panamanian writers include Raúl Leis, Eustorgio Chong Ruiz, Ariel Barria Alvarado, Enrique Jaramillo Levi, and Guillermo Sánchez Borbón, who cowrote the book *In the Time of Tyrants: Panama, 1968-1990*, which is about political corruption in Panama.

*Above:* **Professor Carlos Fuentes (1928– ) is a respected Latin American author. Born in Panama, Fuentes worked as a diplomat for the Mexican government before becoming a writer in the 1950s. He is best known for his novel *La Region Mas Transparente*, or "Where the Air is Clear."**

# Arts

Most of the works of art produced in Panama before its independence were inspired either by European trends or by religious themes. Apart from the various art forms practiced by Panama's native Amerindian populations, distinctively Panamanian art did not really develop until after the country gained independence in 1903. Panama's early West Indian immigrants brought with them African influences that have been incorporated into Panamanian painting, music, and dance.

## Music and Dance

Panamanians listen to many types of music, including salsa, tango, ska, and reggae. Musical styles from Argentina, Colombia, Cuba, and other Caribbean countries have all come together in the melting pot of Panamanian musical tastes. Drums, castanets, bells, and flutes are some instruments Panamanian musicians commonly use. Panamanians also love to dance, and this is evident in the country's numerous nightclubs and bars, where many working-age Panamanians spend their evenings listening to music and dancing with friends. *Tamborito* (TAHM-boh-REE-toh), which means "little drum," is Panama's national dance.

*Left:* Chocolate Genius is a Panamanian-born singer and songwriter based in the United States. His real name is Marc Anthony Thompson. He has released a number of albums, including *Watts and Paris* (1989), *Black Music* (1998), and *Godmusic* (2001).

**PANAMANIAN RHYTHMS: A MIX OF CULTURES**

The music of Panama is a delightful mixture of Amerindian, African, Caribbean, and Spanish influences. Although modern musical styles, such as pop, hip-hop, and rap, are popular in the country, local folk music still holds a special place in the hearts of Panamanians.
*(A Closer Look, page 68)*

*Left:* **Rubén Blades (*left*) and Robert Duvall (*right*) appear in a scene from the film *Assassination Tango* (2002), which Duvall also directed.**

Panamanian-born Rubén Blades (1948– ) is one of Latin America's most famous and well-loved salsa musicians. A multi-talented performer, Blades has not only sung and composed songs and soundtracks but also acted in numerous Hollywood films, including *The Two Jakes* (1990), *Devil's Own* (1997), and *Once Upon a Time in Mexico* (2003). A remarkable individual, Blades also found the time to attend Harvard Law School twice despite his illustrious career in entertainment. He first earned a master's degree and then a doctorate in international law. In 1994, he ran for the presidency in Panama but was unsuccessful.

## Famous Painters

In the course of the twentieth century, a number of Panamanian painters rose to fame and received international recognition for their works. Among these artists is Roberto Lewis (1874-1949), who is best remembered for his series of murals inside the Palace of the Herons, the official residence of Panama's president. Humberto Ivaldi (1909–1947) studied under Lewis before leaving for Madrid, where he studied at the Academia de San Fernando for five years (1930–1935). After returning to Panama, Ivaldi made a name for himself with such works as *Wind on the Hill* (1945) and *Mitzi Arias de Saint Malo* (1947). Ivaldi himself was a mentor to many students, one of whom was Alfredo Sinclair (1915– ), a respected contemporary Panamanian painter.

**LIKE FATHER, LIKE DAUGHTER**

The daughter of Alfredo Sinclair, Olga Sinclair (1957– ) became a painter under the guidance of her father. Olga Sinclair studied in Panama, Madrid, and London as she established a distinct style and a reputation of her own. Like her father, Olga Sinclair has held many individual exhibitions, both in Panama and in other countries.

# Handicrafts

Panama's Amerindian peoples practice many folk arts, including basketry, embroidery, wood carving, and pottery. The Wounaan and Emberá women are famous for their hand-woven baskets, while the Kuna women are admired for their stitchwork. The *mola* (MOU-lah) is the most famous product of the Kuna women. A mola is made by sewing together many layers of cloth using the reverse appliqué technique. "Reverse appliqué" means that the desired pattern or design is first cut out of a piece of fabric. The edges of the cut areas are then folded underneath, and the cut piece of fabric is sewn onto a second, differently colored piece of fabric, so that the design emerges with contrasting colors. This process is repeated several times over until a colorful and intricate design is formed.

The province of Coclé is famous for having a long history in pottery. Pre-Columbian ceramic items, including plates, bowls, and urnlike vessels, were unearthed at Coclé in the early 1900s, and experts marvel at their exceptionally high quality. The ceramic pieces found in Coclé were also decorated with colorful

*Below:* **Examples of mola stitchwork hang on display to attract potential buyers.**

and distinctive intricate designs involving geometric shapes or drawings of people and animals. Today, the town of La Peña, in the province of Veraguas, is famous as a commercial producer of pre-Columbian-style clay products.

The Wounaan and Emberá Amerindians are also known to produce *tagua* (TAH-gwah) carvings. Tagua nuts are dried palm seeds that require great skill to carve. Tagua nuts are approximately the size of golf balls and are so hard that they have been called "vegetable ivory." Also known as "ivory nuts," tagua nuts are carved into miniature sculptures. Often decorated with vegetable dyes, tagua carvings have, in recent years, gained greater recognition through the work of several local and international organizations such as the Panamá Audubon Society, the Bernheim Gallery in Panama City, the Smithsonian Tropical Research Institute (STRI), and the United Nations Educational, Scientific, and Cultural Organization (UNESCO).

The provinces of Herrara and Los Santos are especially famous for making the *pollera* (pou-YEH-rah), the national dress of Panama, and also the elaborate accessories, such as headpieces, hair ornaments, and necklaces, that accompany the outfit.

## HANDICRAFTS: A NEW WAY OF LIVING

Making handicrafts that are typically sold to tourists (*left*) is an increasingly important trade for Panama's various Amerindian groups for two main reasons. First, many Panamanian Amerindians are no longer able to rely wholly on the natural environments in which they live to survive. Unable to produce enough food through farming, hunting, or fishing, many of Panama's Amerindians have turned to selling their handicrafts so that they can buy food and other necessities. Second, making handicrafts is also a way for Panama's Amerindian groups to ensure that this part of their culture will be passed on to younger generations.

## THE POLLERA: PANAMA'S NATIONAL DRESS

Panamanians regard the pollera as a symbol of their country. Panamanian women wear their national dresses with pride during festivals and special occasions.

(A Closer Look, page 70)

# Leisure and Festivals

## How Panamanians Relax

Panamanians are a warm and sociable people, and this is especially evident in the way they welcome and treat foreign visitors. As is the case with many Latin American countries, family ties in Panama are usually strong, making family-oriented activities popular with Panamanians.

Many Panamanians enjoy outdoor activities. Some people favor spending their free time at the local beaches, where they can sunbathe, surf, snorkle, or scuba dive, while others prefer to take in what nature has to offer by hiking or camping in the country's many nature reserves or national parks. For a weekend getaway, some Panamanians visit their extended family members in the countryside, where they can both escape from the city and be close to relatives.

For those who remain in the country's cities during weekends, shopping at any of the numerous malls, watching a movie, and eating out are some of the more common forms of recreation. Located near the Panama Canal, the Amador

*Below:* **In Panama, men often gather in groups to play dominoes.**

Causeway is a popular destination during weekends and holidays among people who live in the capital city. A narrow strip of land connecting three small islands — Naos, Perico, and Flamenco — the Amador Causeway is where many Panamanians go to walk, jog, skate, or cycle in humanmade but picturesque surroundings.

*Above:* **Panamanians have many beaches to choose from on the country's generous coastline.**

## Spending Time with Family

At home, Pananamians try as often as possible to gather for daily meals, over which family members may share their day's experiences with one another. Many Panamanian families also watch television together to relax.

The basic family unit in Panama typically consists of parents and their children. While some Panamanian children live with both their parents and grandparents, who usually help look after younger members of the household, single-parent families are also common in the country.

Panamanians make it a point to attend family gatherings and celebrations of special occasions such as birthdays, anniversaries, baptisms, and marriages. Celebratory events usually involve music, dancing, food, and a lot of lively conversation.

# Sports

Panamanians play a wide variety of sports, including basketball, soccer, and tennis, but they love baseball most of all. Baseball is not only played throughout the country, but it is also a popular spectator sport. More than forty Panamanians have played professional baseball in North America since the 1950s.

Basketball is another popular sport that has drawn many Panamanian fans. The country has a number of regional teams and also a national team. The Panamanian national basketball team has played in tournaments such as the Tour of the Americas (2001) and Centrobasket (1999 and 2001). Jair Peralta, Alfonso Johnson, Eric Cadenas, and Antonio Garcia are some members of Panama's national basketball team.

Soccer has a moderate but growing following in Panama, where teams including Árabe Unido, Panamá Viejo, Plaza Amador, Sporting 89, and Tauro play the sport. In December 2003, the Fédération Internationale de Football Association (FIFA) ranked the Panamanian national soccer team 125th in the world. Interest in soccer significantly increased in Panama after October 2002, when the Panamanian team qualified for the FIFA World Youth Championship.

## BOXING LEGENDS

Panama has produced a number of boxing champions over the years. Roberto Durán, Ismael Laguna, and Eusebio Pedroza are a few of the country's boxing greats.
*(A Closer Look, page 46)*

*Left:* **Members of the Panamanian national baseball team congratulate one another after beating the Brazilian team 7-0 in the 2002 Intercontinental Baseball Cup competition held in Havana, Cuba.**

For fitness and leisure, many Panamanians practice sporting activities such as jogging, swimming, snorkling, horseback riding, cycling, hunting, and fishing. Cockfights and horse races are popular spectator sports in the country, and some thrill-seeking Panamanians enjoy betting on these events. A legacy of the Spanish colonial years, bullfights in Panama today are performed mainly at festivals. Bullfighting as a sport is not taken too seriously in Panama, and bullfights in the country do not involve killing the bulls.

*Above:* **Panamanians generally enjoy outdoor recreational activities, including kayaking. Here, the people are paddling along the Chagres River in the province of Colón.**

## Panamanians in Professional Baseball

Born in Panama, Rodney Cline Carew (1945– ), better known as Rod Carew, grew up to become a baseball legend both in Panama and in the United States. In 1962, Carew moved to New York City, and by 1967, he was playing for the Minnesota Twins. In 1979, he began playing for the California Angels (present-day Anaheim Angels). Carew retired in 1986 and still enjoys a good reputation as one of the best hitters in the history of baseball. Mariano Rivera (New York Yankees), Bruce Chen (Atlanta Braves), Einar Diaz (Texas Rangers), and Carlos Lee (Chicago White Sox) are some of the more recent Panamanian faces in North American professional baseball.

*Left:* **Some pious Roman Catholic Panamanians reenact the trial and crucifixion of Jesus Christ on Good Friday each year.**

## CARNIVAL AND OTHER FESTIVALS

**Carnival, the National Flower and Coffee Festival, and the Festival of the Black Christ are some of the most important festival celebrations in Panama.**
*(A Closer Look, page 50)*

# Religious Festivals

Many religious festivals are celebrated in Panama each year. Because Roman Catholic and Protestant Panamanians form a vast majority of the country's population, most of the religious festivals observed in the country are related to Christianity. Carnival is a festival celebrated in many places around the world. In Panama, Canival celebrations are usually spread over four days before Ash Wednesday, which can fall in February or March. The festivities begin on Saturday morning and finish with a dawn celebration on Ash Wednesday. People then return home to rest.

Many Panamanians also observe Holy Week, which consists of the days before Jesus Christ was crucified and ends with Easter Sunday. Holy Week in Panama is marked by dance and drama performances, as well as by processions on Good Friday. Certain religious festivals vary in importance from region to region. In Portobelo, for example, the Festival of Cristo Negro, or Black Christ, held in October, is the key annual event, while Corpus Christi is of greater significance in Los Santos. Corpus Christi takes place in June.

*Below:* **Roman Catholic Panamanian children carry crosses as they make their way through the streets of Panama City as part of a Good Friday procession.**

# Secular Holidays and Festivals

Panamanians celebrate their country's independence twice a year — on November 3, which marks the country's independence from Colombia, and also on November 28, which marks the country's freedom from Spain. Mother's Day in Panama is a national holiday. It falls on December 8, which is also the day of the Immaculate Conception according to the Roman Catholic calendar.

The Festival Nacional de la Mejorana, or the National Folkloric Festival of La Mejorana, takes place every September in the city of Guararé. Established in 1949 by Professor Manuel F. Zárate, the festival aims to preserve and promote Panamanian folk culture. Every year, Panamanians and tourists gather in Guararé to learn about traditional Panamanian life and customs through a series of performances involving folk musical instruments, singing, dancing, and bullfighting. People who come to Guararé for the festival can also watch an oxcart parade.

Every July, residents of the city of Las Tablas celebrate the day of the city's patron saint, Sanda Librada, with the Festival de la Pollera. During this festival, Panamanian women from all over the country gather in Las Tablas to show their versions of the national dress to visitors. The polleras on display are heavily decorated, and the decorations are often painstakingly detailed.

**CENTENNIAL CELEBRATIONS IN 2003**

November 3 marks the day Panama declared its independence from Colombia and became a republic. In 2003, November 3 marked one hundred years of independence for the country.
*(A Closer Look, page 52)*

*Left:* Panamanian schoolchildren wave their country's flag during Independence Day celebrations on November 3.

39

# Food

## Mixed Influences

Traditional Panamanian dishes are characteristically aromatic
and flavorful and reflect a mix of Amerindian, Spanish, and
African influences. In fact, nowhere in Panamanian cooking is
this mixed heritage more apparent than in the wide variety of
staple foods that the locals eat. Rice, legumes, beans, corn,
yams, cassava, and plantains are some Panamanian staples.

A classic Panamanian dish, *sancocho* (sahn-KOH-shoh) is
essentially a hearty chicken-and-vegetable soup. To prepare
sancocho, chicken is boiled in water with some onions, green
peppers, corn, and yams and flavored with salt, oregano,
and culantro, which is a fragrant relative of cilantro. Recipes
for sancocho may vary slightly from region to region in the
country, but it is always served and eaten with steamed rice.

*Tamale* (tah-MAHL) is another favorite dish in Panama.
To make tamale, dough made of cornmeal, is portioned and
stuffed with a mixture of chicken or pork and some vegetables.
Each portion is then wrapped with a banana leaf and molded
into a square shape. The parcels are either boiled or broiled.

*Left:* **Because the
country has access
to plentiful seafood,
dishes such as grilled
fish (*far right*) or a
crayfish cocktail (*center
bottom*), are common
in restaurants.**

Left: Panama City has a variety of restaurants that serve not only local favorites but also international fare and grilled meats.

Because of the country's location, Panamanians generally eat a lot of seafood. *Ceviche* (seh-VEE-sheh) is a popular Panamanian appetizer. Served chilled, ceviche involves soaking pieces of raw fish in a marinade of lemon or lime juice, chopped onions, salt, pepper, and olive oil for about twenty-four hours before serving it with crackers on the side. Some makers of ceviche use cooked shrimp instead of raw fish. *Fufu* (FOO-FOO) is another famous Panamanian seafood dish. Pieces of plantains, yams, and fried fish are cooked in coconut milk before being served with a spicy sauce.

## Side Dishes and Snacks

In Panama, plantains are used to make not only filling staple foods but also tasty snacks and side dishes. For a simple, savory snack, Panamanians fry sliced plantains until they turn golden brown, mash the slices up, add some salt, and then refry the mashed plantains until they become crisp. Plantains cooked in butter and sugar and flavored with powdered cinnamon or nutmeg is a side dish popular with Panamanians. Sometimes cheese is used instead of cinnamon or nutmeg. Another favorite side dish is *arroz con guando* (ah-ROHS con GUAN-doh), which is made from cooking rice and beans in coconut milk. *Hojaldras* (ou-HAHL-drahs) is a flat piece of fried dough that most people eat at breakfast and some people eat for a snack. Nicknamed the "Panamanian donut," hojaldras is often eaten with sugar.

### FAVORITE DRINKS

*Chicheme* (shi-SHE-mei) is a drink made by cooking cornmeal with water, sugar, and cinnamon. The wide variety of tropical fruits, such as papayas and pineapples, available in the country is used to make refreshing *chichas* (CHEE-chas). Chichas are made by mixing fruit juices with water and sugar, and they are served chilled or topped with ice.

### SWEET TREATS

Because of the tropical climate, *raspado* (rahs-PAH-dou) is one of Panama's most popular sweet treats. A raspado is a cone of crushed ice topped with a variety of syrups and sweetened, condensed milk. *Cocadas* (koh-KAH-dahs) are a type of coconut-flavored candy, and *quequis* (KEH-kihs) are cookies made from flour, coconut, honey, and ginger spices.

# A CLOSER LOOK AT PANAMA

The isthmus of Panama is too often overshadowed by the Panama Canal. The canal, indeed, provides much of the country's resources and is a historic piece of engineering, but the diverse natural environments on the isthmus are no less intriguing. The Darién Jungle, for example, which UNESCO declared a World Heritage site and later a biosphere reserve, is home to some of the world's oldest tropical forests. In addition to the Darién Jungle, Panama is also home to numerous national parks and nature reserves. The Talamanca Range-La Amistad Reserves, in particular, have a unique collection of plants and

*Opposite:* **Four Chocó Amerindian children float on a traditional-style boat.**

animals that are products of cross-breeding between North and South American species. Two endangered species, the West Indian manatee and the Harpy eagle, inhabit Panamanian territory.

The Panamanian people, from the country's Amerindian groups to the larger mestizo population, have a wide variety of vibrant cultural practices. Panama's religious festivals, such as Carnival and the Festival of the Black Christ, are spectacular events. The centennial of Panama's independence, November 3, 2003, was probably the most significant secular event in recent times.

*Above:* **A Kuna Amerindian living on one of the San Blas Islands sits outside his thatched-roof hut.**

# Amerindians in Panama

## The Kuna

The Kuna Amerindians historically inhabited central Panama and some of the nearby San Blas Islands. Today, most of the Kuna population is divided among the Kuna Yala Comarca, a reserve protected under Panamanian laws, and a small fraction of the San Blas Islands. Located on the Caribbean coast of mainland Panama, the Kuna Yala Comarca is a narrow strip of land bordered by Colombia to the east and the province of Colón to the west.

The Kuna were a powerful and important tribe before the Spanish arrived. They had an organized society. In the sixteenth century, each Kuna village was headed by a chief, who either led his village to fight and conquer other villages or united with other Kuna village chiefs in wars against neighboring Amerindian tribes, such as the Chocó. Within Kuna society, a class structure divided the people.

*Below:* **Kuna women traditionally wear long skirts and blouses that feature mola-style decorations on the front and back. Many Kuna women paint black lines down the centers of their noses.**

44

The structure of Kuna society eventually collapsed with the arrival of the Spanish. Kuna religious practices also changed with Western influences. In the twenty-first century, the Kuna in Panama live in small villages and lead mainly agricultural lives. They also fish and hunt.

## The Guaymí

The Guaymí Amerindians inhabit western Panama, and the languages they speak belong to the Chibchan family, which also includes the languages of the Kuna Amerindians. The Guaymí are divided into two main groups — the Northern Guaymí and the Southern Guaymí. Although both groups practice agriculture, the Northern Guaymí also depend heavily on hunting and gathering in the forests for their food supplies, while the Southern Guaymí are generally more agricultural but also gather edible wild plants in addition to growing their food crops. The Guaymí people, especially the Southern Guaymí, cultivate a wide variety of food crops, which include staples such as corn, cassava, plantains, beans, papayas, and bananas. Fishing is the main hunting activity of the Southern Guaymí. Guaymí villages consist of huts with thatched roofs, and the Guaymí people engage in crafts such as basket weaving, net making, and pottery.

## THE CHOCÓ

The Chocó Amerindians inhabit the lowland areas in present-day Panama and Colombia. The Chocó population is composed of two main groups — the Northern Chocó and the Southern Chocó. Panama is home to the Northern Chocó, who are the larger of the two groups. In Panama, the Chocó tend to concentrate along the lower reaches of rivers that empty into the Gulf of San Miguel, and Chocó housing typically consists of circular huts on stilts. The Chocó grow food crops and hunt animals to eat. Chocó hunters either use bows and arrows or poison darts shot out of blowguns to hunt animals. In a Chocó home, the oldest male acts as the spokesman of the household.

The Chocó fought several legendary battles against the Kuna Amerindians and the invading Spanish forces in the 1600s.

# Boxing Legends

## Ismael Laguna (1943– )

Born in Colón, Ismael Laguna won the world lightweight championship twice during his boxing career. He entered professional boxing when he turned seventeen, and in 1965, he defeated Puerto Rican Carlos Ortiz to win the World Boxing Association (WBA) championship less than three months before he turned twenty-two. In 1970, Laguna defeated Mexican Armando Ramos to win his second world championship title. Before he retired in 1972, fans and admirers of Laguna's quick reflexes and solid punches called him *El Tigre de Santa Isabel*, which means "the Tiger of Santa Isabel."

## Roberto Durán (1951– )

Nicknamed *Mano de Piedra*, which means "stone hand," Roberto Durán became a professional boxer at sixteen. Despite not having any formal training, Durán managed to win twenty-one fights in a row. His natural talent for the sport impressed businessman Carlos Eleta, who supported Durán's boxing career. In 1972, Durán won his first world title in the lightweight division, defeating Ken Buchanan of Scotland. In 1980, Durán defeated

*Left:* Panamanian Ismael Laguna (*right*) and Puerto Rican Carlos Ortiz (*left*) fought a rematch in August 1967. Laguna lost the match.

American Sugar Ray Leonard in the welterweight division for his second world title. Durán's career in professional boxing was long and illustrious. He retired in 2002 at the age of fifty. Durán remains a legendary sporting figure in Panama. He is one of few boxers in the world to have competed and won world championship titles in different weight divisions, including junior middleweight (1983) and middleweight (1989).

*Above:* **Durán (*left*) and Sugar Ray Leonard (*right*) celebrate Durán's victory over Davey Moore in 1983, in which Durán won the WBA Junior Middleweight crown.**

## Eusebio Pedroza (1953– )

Born in Panama City, Pedroza became a professional boxer in 1973. He started his boxing career in the bantamweight division but was only slightly successful until he entered the heavier featherweight division. In 1978, Pedroza beat Spaniard Cecilio Lastra to win the WBA championship in the featherweight division. Described as an aggressive, hard punching fighter, Pedroza maintained an impressive career record. Of the forty-nine matches in which he competed, Pedroza won forty-two of them, with twenty-five ending in knockouts.

# The Bridge of the Americas

## A Canal of Separation

The construction of the Panama Canal required dramatic changes to the physical landscape of Panama. The most important of them was the division of the isthmus into two parts in order to allow vessels to move back and forth between the Pacific Ocean and the Caribbean Sea. Dividing the isthmus required that millions of cubic feet (cubic meters) of rock and earth had to be dug up and removed. The large-scale excavation divided not only the isthmus but also the continents of North and South America.

The Panama Canal opened in 1914, and the isthmus remained split for about half a century. No safe way for people to travel between the eastern and western halves of the isthmus existed until Maurice Thatcher, a member of the Isthmian Canal Commission and one-time civil governor of the Canal Zone,

*Below:* **The Bridge of the Americas was first known as the Thatcher Ferry Bridge, named after Maurice Thatcher (1870–1973). At the official opening ceremony of the bridge, Thatcher was the guest of honor who cut the tape. Thatcher, a U.S. congressman, lived longer than any other member of the Isthmian Canal Commission.**

created a cross-canal ferry service. Called the Thatcher Ferry, it operated for some thirty years. Although the service is no longer in operation, docks for the closed-down ferry service still stand on both sides of the canal.

*Above:* **Ships that are either entering or leaving the Panama Canal sail under the bridge.**

## Relinking Separate Continents

On December 23, 1958, a ceremony was held to declare U.S. commitment to relinking the two halves of the isthmus with a bridge. The Panamanian president at the time, Ernesto de la Guardia Jr., and then-U.S. ambassador Julian Harrington were among the important people who attended the ceremony. Construction of the bridge began in 1959. The bridge was completed two and a half years later at a cost of U.S. $20 million. On October 12, 1962, the bridge, which was known then as the Thatcher Ferry Bridge, was formally opened. The arched steel structure that joins the isthmus's two parts measures about 5,476 feet (1,669 m) long. Four lanes of traffic, two in each direction, and sidewalks on both sides of the highway span the length of the bridge. The bridge is suspended at a height of about 387 feet (118 m).

# Carnival and Other Festivals

## Carnival

Panama's Carnival celebrations are among the largest in the world, rivaling those held in Rio de Janeiro, Brazil or in New Orleans, Louisiana, where the festival is known as Mardi Gras. Carnival is a Roman Catholic tradition that marks the time before Lent, the traditionally somber period of forty days between Ash Wednesday and Easter during which Roman Catholics are supposed to abstain from meat. In Panama, Carnival celebrations begin as early as the Friday before Ash Wednesday. During this period, a festive spirit grips the nation. Beginning on Friday, Panamanian Carnival festivities and partying intensify with each passing day. They peak on Tuesday, when the largest of the street parades take place. Most businesses are closed during Carnival.

Located about 130 miles (209 km) west of Panama City, the city of Las Tablas is widely thought to be the best place in the country to witness and participate in Carnival celebrations. Floats and costumes are decorated to the last inch, and much dancing and feasting takes place on almost every street.

*Above:* **Dubbed the Queen of the 1995 Panamanian Carnival, this woman in an elaborate costume waves to onlookers from her float.**

*Left:* **These children dance during the Carnival parade held in Panama City in 1998.**

50

## The Festival of the Black Christ

The Festival of Cristo Negro, or Black Christ, is held annually in Portobelo and is one of Panama's most anticipated religious festivals. The Black Christ is a large statue of Jesus Christ carved out of dark wood. A small, rural coastal town for most of the year, Portobelo comes alive with the procession of the Black Christ every October 21.

To attend the procession, crowds of Panamanian worshippers from throughout the country make their way to the historic town of Portobelo, often on foot. There, they honor and thank Jesus Christ by observing and taking part in a procession with the Black Christ statue. The procession itself involves about eighty men shouldering a heavy pedestal on which the statue has been placed and then walking through the narrow streets of Portobelo. The procession takes hours to complete because the men move slowly, taking one step back after every two steps forward. Hundreds of worshippers holding lit candles follow the men carrying the Black Christ. The procession — and the Black Christ's jouney — ends at a church.

### NATIONAL FLOWER AND COFFEE FESTIVAL

Located in Panama's westernmost province of Chiriquí, Boquete is where the National Flower and Coffee Festival is held every January. Despite being in the tropics, Boquete has an average annual temperature of about 68° F (20° C) because of the region's generally higher altitudes. The fertile slopes of Boquete are conducive to the growing of lucrative export crops, such as flowers, coffee, citrus fruits, and strawberries. Boquete is believed to produce the best coffee in Panama, while the fields of lilies, hibiscus, roses, hortenses, carnations, orchids, and sunflowers give Boquete's landscape incredible color and beauty when they bloom.

# Centennial Celebrations in 2003

## One Century Old

November 3, 2003, marked the one hundredth year Panama has been an independent republic. To ensure that this momentous event was suitably marked in Panamanian history, President Moscoso created the National Centennial Committee to organize activities aimed both at commemorating the nation's independence and celebrating the country's people and culture. The committee planned numerous civic and cultural activities for the whole year.

## Fireworks, Music, and More

The centennial celebrations officially began on the night of November 2 at ten o'clock. A candlelight vigil was held, and 100,000 candles were given out to the people who lined Balboa Avenue in Panama City. Members of Panama's national security forces then marched through the capital city's main streets carrying torches and the country's flag to the Independence Plaza in the Historic District of Panama City. President Moscoso

*Left:* Panamanians watch a spectacular fireworks display light up the sky over the Metropolitan Cathedral in Panama City.

*Left:* Crowned in 2002, Justine Pasek was initially the runner-up in the Miss Universe pageant but won the pageant by default after the first-place contestant, Russian Oxana Fedorova, withdrew from her pageant duties.

## CENTENNIAL ART

Panama's artists received special recognition during the centennial celebrations. The Museum of Contemporary Art organized an exhibition titled "One Hundred Years of Art in Panama," in which nearly 130 works by Panama's most important artists were shown to the public.

received the flag and gave a speech. At the stroke of midnight, bells in churches throughout the country were rung, and a fireworks display, as well as music and singing, followed.

At eight o'clock the next morning, church bells throughout the nation chimed again, and a Christian religious ceremony was held. At nine o'clock, a parade with a patriotic theme moved through the main streets of Panama City. Many of the spectators waved the Panamanian flag. Some women wore the country's national dress, the pollera. The day's most anticipated event, however, did not start until six o'clock in the evening. The Centennial Concert, which featured both local and international celebrities, lasted until midnight.

On November 4, more parades filled the capital city's streets. School marching bands played traditional and patriotic tunes, while a series of floats led by Justine Pasek, who, in 2002, became the first Panamanian to win the Miss Universe pageant, represented Panama's provinces and diverse local cultures.

## GUESTS OF HONOR

Apart from visits by Hollywood personalities such as Bruce Willis and Sean Connery, fourteen presidents and numerous other dignitaries paid official visits to Panama during this centennial celebration. U.S. secretary of state Colin Powell represented the United States, while other leaders, such as Taiwan president Chen Shui-bian, represented their respective peoples.

# The Darién Jungle

Panama's easternmost province of Darién is the country's largest but also its least inhabited region. Dense tropical forests cover most of the province, and the region is not readily accessible. In fact, the Darién region is the only gap in the Pan-American Highway, the road system that was intended to stretch continuously from Alaska to Tierra del Fuego, in southernmost Chile.

## The Darién National Park

Panama's largest national park, at about 2.1 million acres (859,333 hectares) in area, Darién National Park consists of diverse landscapes, including sandy beaches, rocky coasts, mangrove swamps, and tropical forests. The park's animal life is also diverse and is being preserved by much vigorous conservation work. In 1981, UNESCO declared the Darién National Park a World Heritage site for Tropical Forests. Two years later, UNESCO named the Darién region a biosphere reserve.

*Below:* **The Darién forests are home to more than 400 native animal species and 2,250 native plant species. More than thirty of these native animal species are threatened. The white-winged guan (***Penelope albipennis***) and the Tumaco seedeater (***Sporophila insulata***) are two critically endangered bird species, and the brown-head spider monkey (***Ateles geoffroyi fusciceps***) and the Gorga's rice rat (***Oryzomys gorgasi***) are critically endangered mammal species.**

Authorities overseeing the national park have agreed to put aside a fraction of the land that they have classified as transition areas. Transition areas are the areas in which some of the humans that inhabit the Darién region live. While the park's core areas extend for about 836,025 acres (338,335 ha), transition areas cover about 460,913 acres (186,529 ha).

## Deforestation in Darién

Deforestation is threatening the purity and survival of Darién's untouched forests. The growing population in the Darién region is one of the main threats to the forests. In 2000, an estimated 31,400 people lived in the Darién region. Small plots of forest near the park's western border have already been cleared for the purpose of farming. With increased deforestation comes many environmental problems, such as soil erosion and the disruption of ecological processes that used to maintain a natural harmony. For example, cutting down trees causes losses of habitats for some animals, which, in turn, cause a break in the food chain when they either move elsewhere to seek shelter or, worse, gradually die out. In addition, the introduction of modern ways and technologies, such as motor vehicles and machinery, to the Darién environment is likely to alter the traditional practices of the land's indigenous peoples and cause dismay among anthropologists.

### CONSERVATION AND DEVELOPMENT

A combination of foreign organizations, such as the World Wildlife Fund (WWF), and local organizations, such as Panama's Association for the Conservation of Nature (ANCON), have been working for years to prevent the Darién region from extensive environmental damage. Shared aims among the various organizations include creating public awareness about the importance of preserving Darién's untouched tropical forests, creating sustainable development for the region through ecologically mindful management of the region's natural resources, and preventing the dilution of centuries-old Amerindian cultures and practices. Ecotourism is one way of promoting sustainable development in the Darién region.

# Manatees: A Dying Breed

## Gentle Nomads

Manatees are extremely gentle creatures. Some scientists have concluded from brain research that manatees have little to no capacity for anger or fear. Although manatees are mostly herbivorous, or plant-eating, animals, some observers have reported seeing a manatee eat an occasional fish. Manatees are nomadic, and they are classified as "semisocial," which means that they are found both in herds and alone. The bond between a manatee mother and her calf, however, is very strong and can last over two years. Manatee mothers are also known to adopt orphaned manatee calves.

Only four species of manatees still exist in the world today. The West Indian manatee (*Trichechus manatus*) is the species found in Panama's waters. By the late twentieth century, manatees had

*Below:* **Apart from the West Indian manatee, the three other species of manatees that still exist are the Amazonian manatee (*Trichecus inunguis*), the West African manatee (*Trichechus senegalensis*), and the dugong (*Dugong dugon*).**

nearly vanished from the country's waters, with only between forty-two and seventy-two left. Usually living in the waters off Panama's northern coast, manatees favor the areas near the province of Bocas del Toro and the Panama Canal system, including Gatún Lake.

## Threats to Their Survival

Poaching, pollution, and habitat destruction are the main causes of the diminishing of Panama's manatee population. Historically, manatees were hunted by Panama's native peoples for food. Archaeological evidence suggests that Panama's Amerindians who lived between A.D. 500 and 900 ate the meat of manatees, which provided them with a rich source of protein. In the late nineteenth century, manatees were extensively hunted so that the many laborers employed by the Panama Canal project could be fed cheaply and amply. As a result, the manatee population known to the people of Panama virtually disappeared. Today, hunting continues to threaten the country's small population of manatees but to a far smaller degree.

Pollution, however, poses a far greater problem. Human garbage and chemical waste, including pesticides, find their way into manatees' habitats and poison not only the manatees but also their food sources. Accidents involving collisions with boats or larger vessels also kill manatees.

**EFFORTS AT CONSERVATION**

Manatees are protected by law in Panama. Conservationist organizations have tried to protect the manatee by establishing marine reserves, but these efforts have not yet succeeded.

# Maritime Services

## The World's Largest Ship Registry

Panama is home to the world's largest ship registry. Established in 1925, Panama's ship registry is also one of the world's oldest. Toward the end of the twentieth century, nearly one-fifth of the world's commercial vessels were registered with Panama. The majority of these vessels, about 60 percent, were Japanese-owned, while about 30 percent were Greek-owned.

The Panamanian ship registry is attractive for a number of reasons. First, it is open to applicants of any nationality, regardless of where their businesses are based. Second, vessels of any size, ranging from container ships to luxury yachts to trawlers, are welcome to register with the Panamanian registry, as long as they fulfill basic safety and environmental requirements. Third, the Panamanian registry does not impose an income tax on ships taking part in international trade.

*Below:* **Three fishers in their boat are dwarfed by a passing cargo ship sailing toward the southern end of the Panama Canal.**

*Left:* **A cargo ship loaded with containers is about to exit the Panama Canal and sail into the Pacific Ocean. Panama charges a toll to each ship passing through the canal. The amount of the charge depends on the weight of the ship.**

In 1958, Panama became a member of the International Maritime Organization (IMO). The IMO is a branch of the United Nations (U.N.) that is focused on raising the standards of maritime safety and environmental practices. At the beginning of the twenty-first century, Panama provided nearly 16 percent of the IMO's budget, making it the world's single largest contributor. Japan was second, providing more than 5 percent of the budget, and the United States was third, at just over 4 percent.

## Ports of Call — From Public to Private

Panama has a number of ports dotting the coasts of the isthmus. Almirante, Cristóbal, and Colón are some of the ports on the country's northern Caribbean coast, while Balboa and La Palma are ports situated along the country's southern Pacific coast. Panama's ports used to be publicly run and supervised by the National Port Authority, which is an agency of the Panamanian government. The privatization of some of Panama's ports began in the 1990s and drew the investments of large corporations, such as Hutchison Whampoa, of Hong Kong; Evergreen, of Taiwan; and the Stevedoring Services of America. Hutchison Whampoa currently operates the ports of Cristobal and Balboa, while the Stevedoring Services of America runs the Manzanillo International Terminal, which is located just off the Colón Free Trade Zone. Evergreen is responsible for the services offered at the Colón Container Terminal.

# National Parks and Wonders

With fifteen national parks and a number of nature reserves and wildlife sanctuaries, Panama offers many opportunities for ecotourism and adventures in the wild such as camping, hiking, snorkeling, and rafting.

## La Amistad International Park

La Amistad International Park occupies an area of 990,682 acres (400,929 hectares) and is shared between Panama and Costa Rica. The area, identified as a whole by UNESCO as the Talamanca Range-La Amistad Reserves, was declared a World Heritage site for tropical forests in 1983, and it later became a World Heritage site for natural properties. Tropical rain forests, much of which are very old and untouched by humans, dominate the landscape of the reserve, and there are parts where ice-age glaciers have left visible marks. The Talamanca Range-La Amistad Reserves are home to a diverse population of Amerindians and also a unique collection of plants and animals. The reserve's geographical

### METROPOLITAN NATIONAL PARK

The Metropolitan National Park is located just outside the heart of Panama City and is relatively small, at 655 acres (265 hectares). Despite being only a short distance away from the country's capital city and largest urban center, plant and animal life are rich in the national park. The park's thick tropical forests support some forty species of mammals and more than two hundred species of birds, while the forests have been the site of rain forest research.

*Left:* A party of ecotourists disembarks from a light aircraft on a runway in Panama. Ecotourism is a growing industry in Panama. Unlike other forms of tourism, ecotourism is mindful of nature. Ecotourists engage in activities that do not cause extensive environmental damage. Ecotourism provides national parks and other protected areas with income in the form of tourist dollars without subjecting the environment to devastating commercial or industrial developments.

location and its physical and climatic conditions support the natural cross-breeding processes between certain North and South American species. This cross-breeding contributes to Panama's great biodiversity.

*Above:* **Geese inhabit this body of water in Volcan, which is a small town located in the foothills of Volcán Barú. From the town of Volcan, visitors can scale the western slope of Volcán Barú.**

## Barú Volcano National Park

The Barú Volcano National Park is so scenic that some people have nicknamed the area the "Switzerland of Central America." Known to the locals as Volcán Barú, the Barú Volcano peaks at 11,401 feet (3,475 m), and the national park occupies an area of more than 34,594 acres (14,000 hectares). Although the volcano's summit is usually covered by clouds, there are some clear days during which it is possible to see the Caribbean Sea on one side and the Pacific Ocean on the other from the top of the mountain.

The quetzal (*Pharomachrus mocinno*), a rare fruit-eating tropical bird that is native to Central America, can also be seen in the national park. The quetzal is identified by its plumage, which is bright green on top and red below. Males of the species have long, streaming tail feathers.

# The Panama Canal

## Leading up to August 15, 1914

The idea of constructing a waterway that cuts through the narrow isthmus of Panama to join two great oceans — the Pacific and the Atlantic — first emerged in the sixteenth century. It was not until the twentieth century, however, that the Panama Canal was built.

In the late nineteenth century, a French construction company headed by Ferdinand de Lesseps made the first attempt to dig a canal through Panama. Lesseps failed, despite his success at creating the Suez Canal. Some years later, the U.S. government decided to undertake the project and pledged considerable resources toward its success. The Panama Canal cost the United States U.S. $352 million and took ten years to complete.

The canal officially opened on August 15, 1914. Before then, ships had to sail around the tip of the South American continent in order to travel from the eastern to the western coast of North America. Ships sailing between Europe and eastern Asia or Australia also benefited from shorter traveling distances.

*Below:* **The Pedro Miguel Locks control the southern third of the canal. The vessels shown here** (*bottom right*) **are in the process of being lowered into the waters of the Pacific Ocean over two stages.**

*Left:* The Gaillard Cut is sometimes known as the Culebra Cut and has an average depth of about 42 feet (13 m).

# Inside the Canal

The canal measures about 40 miles (65 km) and consists of three main sections. The northern section is controlled by the Gatún Locks, which close or open to respectively raise or lower the area's water level. For southbound ships, the locks are closed to trap incoming water from the Chagres River, raising the water level to the level of the manmade Gatún Lake, located to the south of the locks. Once the water level is raised, the ships are able to sail from the Gatún Locks to the southern end of the lake, covering a distance of about 23 miles (37 km). For northbound ships, the locks open to lower the ships into the waters of Panama's northern coast.

The middle section includes the Gaillard Cut, which extends for about 8 miles (13 km), and is where ships pass between the North American and South American continental regions. The southern section is controlled by the Pedro Miguel Locks, which function similarly to the Gatún Locks. In this section, southbound ships are lowered into Lake Miraflores from the Gaillard Cut. Two sets of locks control the water level of Lake Miraflores, and southbound ships are lowered from the lake into the Pacific Ocean. Correspondingly, the Pedro Miguel Locks raise northbound ships to the level of the Gaillard Cut so they can continue their journey toward the Caribbean Sea.

## PANAMA DURING WORLD WAR II

Panama's role in World War II was limited and followed U.S. leadership. During the war, the United States established more than 130 defense sites and stationed tens of thousands of soldiers in Panama to protect the canal. Panama regained control of ninety-eight of the sites after the war.

# Panama City

## Old and New Panama

The city of Panamá Vieja, or Old Panama, was founded in 1519 and thrived until 1671, when Welshman Henry Morgan led a devastating attack on the Spanish colony. Morgan was a buccaneer who was known for his raids on Spanish colonies in the Caribbean in the seventeenth century. At the recommendation of Spaniard Alonso Mercado de Villacorta, a new site was chosen for the rebuilding of the colonial city. Three years after the attack, construction of Panamá Nuevo, or New Panama, began about 5 miles (8 km) west of Old Panama. The Panama City of today is what was originally New Panama.

New Panama was built with the intention of recreating the Spanish colonial splendor that characterized parts of Old Panama. New Panama's early colonial buildings, some of which are still standing today, followed the original plan of Old Panama. Today, New Panama is known as the Historic District of Panama City. UNESCO declared it a World Heritage site in 1997. In 2003, UNESCO declared Old Panama a World Heritage site.

*Left:* This three-story tower from a Spanish colonial cathedral is a famous monument of Old Panama that was destroyed in the seventeenth-century pirate attack led by Henry Morgan.

## Panama City

The building and subsequent opening of the Panama Canal in the early twentieth century led Panama City to develop at a rapid pace. Offering port facilities at a strategic geographical location, Panama attracted a variety of businesses. Shipping services, banks, steel mills, timber mills, and breweries soon were part of the country's rising economy. Advanced transportation infrastructure was put in place.

With the building of the Panama Canal, the Panama Railroad, and the Transisthmian and Pan-American highways, Panama truly became the crossroads of the Americas.

In the twenty-first century, Panama City is every bit an ultramodern, cosmopolitan city. Home to numerous skyscrapers; a financial center that is supported by more than one hundred banks; and the sprawling Atlapa Convention Center, which can host up to five thousand people, Panama City is attractive not only to businesspeople but also to vacationers who enjoy staying in the city's many luxury hotels and boutique inns. The city has two shopping districts, Avenida Central and Via Espana.

*Above:* **The skyline of Panama City leaves no doubt that it is an ultramodern urban center.**

# The Panama Railroad

## Inspired by the Search for Gold

In the late 1840s, gold was discovered in California. News of the discovery spurred waves of people to journey to the western United States in search of a richer future. To reach California from the eastern United States, some people followed the traditional routes of either sailing around the southern tip of the South American continent or traveling on land across the North American continent. Many people, however, also came to believe that the most efficient way to reach California from the eastern United States was to first sail south to the northern coast of the isthmus of Panama, trek south across the isthmus, and then sail north to California from the southern coast of the isthmus. Most of those who arrived in Panama, however, had underestimated the treacherous trek across the isthmus. The growing population of fortune-seekers and the increased traffic of both people and U.S. mail through the isthmus convinced the United States government that the Panama Railroad would be profitable. Its construction began in 1850.

**IN THE TWENTY-FIRST CENTURY**

The railway operated for many years under U.S. administration. In 1979, control of the Panama Railroad was turned over to Panama. The railroad gradually fell into disrepair until the late 1990s, when restoration work began. Today, the railroad has been renamed the Panama Canal Railway and is used to transport passengers and cargo between the Atlantic and Pacific coasts, much like it did in the days of the nineteenth-century gold rush.

*Left:* The idea of building a railroad across the isthmus of Panama was first developed by the English in the early 1800s. Numerous obstacles led the English to soon abandon the project, which the French attempted to finish but also later dropped. Toward the end of the nineteenth century, American businessmen gathered sufficient resources to complete the project. The conviction of engineers George W. Totten and John C. Trautwine plus the work — and often the lives — of laborers led to success.

# A Mixed History

The Panama Railroad has a history that is both grim and glorious. The railroad has been called the foundation of the Panama Canal because the canal could not have been consructed without the support of the railroad. Despite some of the problems that stood in the way of building the Canal, such as difficult terrain and tropical diseases, the railroad took only five years — half the time it took to construct the Canal — to complete. The railroad cost U.S. $8 million to build, and its stocks were once the most expensive on the New York Stock Exchange, at U.S. $295 per share.

The darker story of the Panama Railroad involves immense loss of human life, often under tragic circumstances. Although exact figures are not available, as many as 12,000 people are believed to have perished building the "Hell Strip." In fact, so many died over short periods of time that disposing of the dead became difficult for the living. Eventually workers began to preserve the bodies of the dead in barrels that were later sold to medical schools. The money earned from these sales was used to build a hospital near the railroad.

# Panamanian Rhythms: A Mix of Cultures

Folk music in Panama varies slightly from region to region. The country's folk-music styles mix together varying degrees of Amerindian, African, Caribbean, and Spanish influences.

## African-Style Drums

African influence in Panamanian folk music is unmistakable in its use of drums. The *pujador* (POO-hah-dor), *repicador* (reh-pee-CAH-dor), and *caja* (CAH-hah) are three types of native drums. All three of these types of drums are made by stretching pieces of animal hide over the ends of hollowed tree trunks. The caja is short and wide in shape, while the other two are long and narrow. The pujador produces deep sounds, while the repicador produces higher-pitched, chattering sounds. The caja is played with either two sticks or two thick balls. In performances involving all three drums, the repicador is the principle drum.

*Below:* Drums have an important place in Panamanian folk music. In fact, the term "tamborito," which is the name of not only Panama's national dance, but also of the style of music that accompanies the dance, means "little drum."

## Spanish-Style Singing

Spanish influence in Panamanian folk music is most apparent in its singing styles, such as the *copla* (COHP-lah) and the *mejorana* (me-hoh-RAH-nah). Both are gender-specific styles, with women performing the copla and men performing the mejorana. Men who sing the mejorana usually also play the *mejoranera* (me-hoh-rah-NEH-rah), a small five-stringed, guitar-like instrument, to accompany their singing. The *saloma* (sah-LOH-mah) is another Panamanian song style. The saloma is distinctive because it involves falsettos and yodeling.

*Above:* The accordion is widely used in Panamanian music. Osvaldo Ayala, nicknamed "*el escorpión de Paritilla,*" or "the scorpion of Paritilla," is one of Panama's most famous and well-loved accordion players.

## The Accordion

When and how the accordion was first introduced to Panamanian musical culture remains a mystery, but the instrument has certainly become common in nearly all forms of Panama's folk music. One story says that the accordion was brought to Panama by European immigrants in the early 1900s as a cheap alternative to the organ for use in church services.

# The Pollera: Panama's National Dress

## Uncertain Origins

Although no one is sure about the precise origins of the pollera, it is widely thought that the dress was inspired by Spanish fashion trends. Few sources agree, however, when the pollera first emerged in Panama. Most accounts point to a time between the sixteenth and seventeenth centuries. An article published in *Diario de Madrid*, a Spanish newspaper, in 1815 is generally accepted as the earliest known record of the pollera being worn in Panama.

Some researchers suggest that the pollera evolved from house dresses, or dresses worn on a daily basis within the home. Other people have said that the pollera was originally the style of dress of female domestic helpers, such as wet nurses, cooks, and wash ladies, in wealthy homes. Still other accounts say that the pollera, which usually is made from light cotton or linen, was what upper-class women wore during the warm, summer months

*Left:* **Panamanian women rarely wear the pollera without elaborate accessories, such as large hair combs and jewelry, including earrings, necklaces, and bracelets. Accessories to the pollera are usually made from gold and decorated with pearls and crystals. They are designed so that some parts move and shimmer when the wearer walks or dances.**

in temperate Spain and that those women who traveled to Panama began to wear it in the isthmus's hot, tropical climate.

Whatever its origin, the pollera eventually came to be associated with Panama's common people and, more recently, with festivals and special occasions, such as weddings.

## The Parts of the Pollera

The pollera consists of two parts: a top and a long skirt. The top has a boat-neck collar and two overlapping layers of ruffles attached to the bodice. The ruffles are usually embroidered with elaborate patterns and trimmed with intricate lace. The top's collar is also decorated, usually with brightly colored ribbons that gather just below the collarbones in the front and over the shoulder blades at the back. The skirt is long and heavily gathered around the waist. The excess fabric allows the wearer to hold up the skirt on either side and fan it out without exposing her legs. The decorations on the skirt often match those used on the top.

*Above:* **The male counterpart of the pollera is far less elaborate, usually consisting of a shirt with designs printed or embroidered on it and trousers. Accessories for men include a hat and a bag woven from dyed vegetable fibers.**

# Saving the Harpy Eagle

## The National Bird of Panama

A magnificent creature, the Harpy eagle (*Harpia harpyja*) is one of the largest eagle species in the world. The body of an adult Harpy eagle can measure up to 40 inches (101 cm) long, and its wingspan can reach to about 7 feet (2 m). Females of the species are generally larger than their male counterparts. Female Harpy eagles weigh between 14 and 18 pounds (6 and 8 kilograms), while male Harpy eagles weigh between 10 and 16 pounds (4.5 and 7 kg). Harpy eagles can fly at speeds of up to 50 miles per hour (80 km per hour).

The plumage of the Harpy eagle is usually composed of slate black feathers on top and white feathers underneath. Light grey feathers cover the eagle's head. The Harpy eagle also has a band of black feathers just under its neck. Probably the most striking feature of the Harpy eagle is its pair of large clawed feet.

Harpy eagles are carnivorous, or meat-eating, animals and prey mainly on rain forest creatures such as monkeys and sloths. Harpy eagles are also known to eat iguanas and birds. When hunting, a Harpy eagle will swoop down from above and capture its prey using its strong claws, which are so powerful that they can crush its prey's bones and cause instant death.

## Threatened with Extinction

The Harpy eagle is an endangered species, and experts do not know how many of these birds are left in the world. In the mid-1990s, nearly thirty Harpy eagle nests were known in Guyana, Venezuela, and Panama. Deforestation and poaching are the main causes of the dwindling of the world's Harpy eagle population. Because each pair of Harpy eagles requires at least 7 square miles (18 square kilometers) of humid tropical forest to thrive and raise their offspring, deforestation means that Harpy eagles are losing more and more of their natural habitat as time passes. Harpy eagles also have a long reproductive cycle, which makes protecting the species from extinction harder. The egg of a Harpy eagle takes between fifty-three and fifty-six days to hatch, and the offspring becomes sexually mature only after four or five years. Harpy eagles raise one chick at a time.

*Above* and *opposite:*
**Efficient and feared predators, Harpy eagles were named after the Greek mythological figure of the Harpy, a part-woman, part-bird monster with sharp claws that snatched objects and people.**

**CATCHING POACHERS**

Poachers are a serious threat to the survival of the Harpy eagle. Humans hunt Harpy eagles for various reasons. While some people kill the bird for food, others want its feathers for use in religious practices. Because the Harpy eagle is Panama's national bird, poachers of it can be imprisoned and fined if they are caught.

# RELATIONS WITH NORTH AMERICA

Much of Panama's modern history has been shaped by its relations with North America, especially with the United States. In the early twentieth century, the United States helped build the Panama Canal and then exclusively controlled the canal, as well as the land on either side of it, the Canal Zone, for nearly a century. The canal was a vital economic resource, but Panama had no share in the profits it generated. As a result, Panama struggled against the United States for decades over the administration of the canal. The United States officially turned the canal over to Panama in December 1999.

*Opposite:* **This building in Panama once housed the headquarters of the U.S. Southern Command. In 1997, the U.S. Southern Command moved its headquarters to southern Florida.**

In the 1980s, relations between the United States and Panama reached an especially low point because of Manuel Antonio Noriega's dictatorship. Noriega's corrupt administration and links to international drug dealers troubled the United States, which imposed trade sanctions on Panama in 1988 and invaded the country in 1989, after the killing of a U.S. Marine. Democracy in 1990 led to mutual respect between the two countries. In the twenty-first century, trade between Panama and both the United States and Canada has been active. Both North American nations also give economic aid to Panama.

*Above:* **The Goethals Monument stands in front of the Panama Canal's administrative building. The monument was built for George Washington Goethals (1858–1928), who was the chief engineer of the canal.**

# The Hay-Bunau-Varilla Treaty

With U.S. support, Panama declared its independence from Colombia on November 3, 1903. Panama had the support of the United States because earlier talks between the United States and Colombia over the construction and running of the proposed Panama Canal had failed. About two weeks after Panama's declaration of independence, on November 18, 1903, the Hay-Bunau-Varilla Treaty was signed. The treaty gave the United States the piece of Panamanian territory that consisted of the future Panama Canal and the Canal Zone, stretching for 5 miles (8 km) from either bank of the canal. Under the treaty, the United States could use and manage this territory as if it were its own and could occupy it for an indefinite period of time. In return, the United States would pay the Panamanian government U.S. $10 million that year and U.S. $250,000 every year thereafter. Panama's first constitution as a republic complemented the treaty by authorizing the United States to mobilize its military forces in Panama in case of trouble. These early arrangements became a lasting source of tension between the two nations.

*Opposite:* **Mounted on a turntable, this gun can fire a missile about 30 miles (48 km) out to sea. It was installed by the United States to defend the canal during World War II. After the war, the United States transferred ninety-eight of 134 defense sites to Panama but sought to retain the rest. The Panamanian government's initial decision to allow the United States to keep the remaining sites was later reversed by the country's parliament because of mounting public pressure. By 1947, the United States gave up the remaining thirty-six sites.**

*Left:* **William Howard Taft (*front row, far left*) and George Washington Goethals (*second row, far left*); were part of a team of Americans who worked on the canal. Goethals was appointed by President Roosevelt to be the canal's chief engineer. Taft succeeded Roosevelt as president. In total, more than 75,000 people from all over the world came to Panama to work on the canal, which cost the United States U.S. $352 million.**

## U.S. Military Developments in Panama

Since the signing of the Hay-Bunau-Varilla Treaty, power struggles among Panama's politicians led to several incidents of civil unrest and, consequently, economic instability. The United States took military action on several occasions (1908, 1912, 1918, and 1925), and Panamanians grew to resent U.S. presence in the country. In 1931, Arnulfo Arias Madrid led a bloody coup that overthrew the Panamanian government. This led the United States to recognize Panamanian minister to Washington Ricardo Alfaro as Panama's new president. In 1936, the Hull-Alfaro Treaty was signed to appease Panamanians by reducing the scope of U.S. power on the isthmus. In June 1940, Arnulfo Arias became Panama's president. When the United States requested land outside the Canal Zone on which to build defense sites, such as landing fields and warning stations, Arias asked for more money and the transfer of some land to Panama. Arias was overthrown by Panamanian security forces in October 1941, and the Panamanian government transferred all defense sites to the United States after the attack on Pearl Harbor in Hawaii two months later. Tens of thousands of U.S. soldiers were sent to Panama to ensure the security of the canal.

### THE HULL-ALFARO TREATY

This treaty removed the United States's right to intervene in Panama's domestic affairs, increased the amount of money paid annually to Panama for the canal and surrounding zone, and required the United States to build a highway across the isthmus.

# The Panama Canal Treaties

The 1970s saw some improvement in relations between Panama and the United States. During that period, General Omar Torrijos Herrera, Panama's military leader at the time, succeeded in putting pressure on the U.S. government to reconsider its position on the Panama Canal and the Canal Zone. An agreement between the two governments was announced in August 1977, and two new treaties were signed by Torrijos and U.S. president Jimmy Carter the next month. The basic treaty, which is known as the Panama Canal Treaty, guaranteed that the canal's operations would be completely transferred to Panama by December 31, 1999, and that U.S. military bases on the isthmus would be gradually shut down until Panama is free of U.S. military presence. The second treaty, known as the Neutrality Treaty, declared the canal to be neutral territory and open to all in times of peace and war. The Panama Canal Treaties, as they came to be known collectively, came into effect on October 1, 1979, and they nullify all earlier treaties relating to the canal.

## Operation Just Cause

Beginning in the early 1980s, when Colonel Manuel Antonio Noriega Morena seized the nation, relations between Panama and the United States entered a downward spiral. Noriega, who was a former spy for the U.S. Central Intelligence Agency (CIA),

*Left:* A U.S. soldier guards a Panamanian prisoner who was captured during Operation Just Cause.

solidified the dictatorship first established by Torrijos and ruled the isthmus with a corrupt and ruthless iron fist. The Noriega years (1983–1989), which shattered Panama's economy, came to an end when the United States launched an invasion of Panama on December 20, 1989. The United States referred to the invasion as Operation Just Cause.

In the wee hours of the morning on December 20, 1989, U.S. troops descended on Panama City and swiftly defeated most resistance attempts. Chaos followed, however, when businesses in Panama City and Colón became the targets of widespread looting by some Panamanians. As a result, an additional 2,000 U.S. soldiers were sent to Panama to restore order. U.S. president George H. W. Bush explained the need for the invasion by saying that it combated drug trafficking, protected the lives and property of Americans, and restored Panamanian liberties. Between 500 and 600 Panamanians were killed in Operation Just Cause, with about half of that number being civilians. Twenty-three U.S. soldiers were also killed, and hundreds from both countries were injured.

*Above:* Jubilant Panamanians hold up the flags of both Panama and the U.S. to mark the end of the Noriega dictatorship.

## NORIEGA IN JAIL

Noriega was captured during Operation Just Cause and sent to the United States to face charges. During the 1980s, some reports accused Noriega of working with Colombian drug cartels in a drug-trafficking scheme. On April 9, 1992, after a trial that lasted for seven months, Noriega was found guilty of eight charges. On July 10, 1992, he was sentenced to forty years in a U.S. prison.

# U.S.-Panama Economic Relations

Following the opening of the canal, Panama's economy grew to rely heavily on U.S. businesses tied to the administration of the Panama Canal or the Canal Zone. As a result, the trade sanctions imposed by the U.S. government in the late 1980s and the political instability of the time harmed Panama's economy greatly. During that period (1987–1989), Panama's gross domestic product (GDP) decreased by 25 percent. By the time the U.S. invasion was over, Panama's economy had come to a virtual standstill because parts of Panama City — the commercial heart of the country — were severely damaged by the fighting. Looting was widespread. Losses were estimated in the hundreds of millions of dollars.

Under the leadership of President Guillermo Endara — and with financial support from the United States — the newly democratic Panamanian government brought about impressive economic recovery in the first half of the 1990s. In 1990, the U.S. Congress approved more than U.S. $420 million in aid to Panama. The money, which made Panama the largest recipient of foreign aid in Latin America in that year, was divided between rebuilding the country's shattered economy and developing a better and

*Below:* **Part of U.S. conglomerate Citigroup, Citibank first established itself in Panama in 1904. Today, Citibank in Panama services nearly 60,000 accounts and employs more than 400 people.**

safer Panamanian society. For much of the 1990s, U.S. aid to the country dwindled with each passing year, and in 1997, Panama received less than U.S. $5 million from the United States. Since President Mireya Moscoso came to power in 1999, however, Panama began receiving more and more assistance from the United States — U.S. $17 million in 1999, U.S. $19.1 million in 2000, and U.S. $24.1 million in 2001.

In the early twenty-first century, the United States is Panama's largest trading partner. In 2001, the United States bought nearly half of Panama's exports, which amounted to about U.S. $398 million worth of goods. In return, Panama buys the largest share of its imports from the United States. In 2000, U.S. products, including crude oil, foodstuffs, and consumer goods, made up more than one-third of Panama's imports, totaling about U.S. $1.8 billion. In 2003, Panamanian president Mireya Moscoso and U.S. president George W. Bush discussed the possibility of creating a Free Trade Agreement (FTA) between the two nations.

*Above:* **In 1906, Panama and Cuba became the world's first two countries to have factories that bottled Coca-Cola outside of the United States. Today, the Coca-Cola company's Panamanian office is known as Coca-Cola de Panama.**

# The Peace Corps in Panama

The Peace Corps first began work in Panama in 1963 but withdrew after about eight years, in 1971. After nearly two decades of absence, the Peace Corps reentered Panama in 1990, and it has worked in the country continuously ever since. In 2003, the Peace Corps had 132 volunteers working on the isthmus. In total, more than 1,300 Americans have served as volunteers for the Peace Corps in Panama. Today, Peace Corps volunteers in Panama work on three main programs: the Community Economic Development Program, the Community Environmental Education Program, and the Agroforestry Extension Program.

# U.S. Influence in Panama

For nearly one century — from the start of the canal's construction to the official handover of the canal's administration to Panamanian authorities in 1999 — thousands of U.S. government officials, military personnel, and civilians have lived and worked in Panama. As a result, the influence of U.S. culture is evident in many areas of Panamanian life, including everyday speech and popular tastes in music, food, and sports.

English words and U.S. figures of speech often find their way into the conversations of Panamanians. In fact, English is taught as a second language in most schools, while some private schools teach in Spanish and English almost equally.

*Left:* **A couple provides food and drinks for U.S. soldiers patrolling the streets in Panama. In 1989, the United States invaded Panama to arrest dictator Manuel Antonio Noriega, who was later convicted of racketeering, drug trafficking, and money laundering.**

U.S. culture has also seeped into Panamanian society through cable television. Some older Panamanians watch cable news broadcasts from the United States, while younger Panamanians watch cable television to keep up with the trends in popular music, fashion, and movies.

U.S. fast-food chains, such as McDonald's, Wendy's, and KFC, are well represented in Panama's urban centers, and many Panamanians frequently eat in them. Panamanians' liking for sports such as baseball and basketball also clearly reflects U.S. influence.

## Panamanians in the United States

Panamanians who travel to the United States are usually there to conduct business, visit family members, or pursue higher education. Some U.S. institutions of higher education have campuses in Panama and run student exchange programs. Florida State University has been operating in Panama for over forty years. The institution provides an opportunity for Panamanians and other Latin Americans to obtain a U.S. education close to their homes. Compared to other Central or Latin American countries, the number of Panamanians who have migrated to the United States is relatively low. The U.S. Census Bureau has estimated that about 100,000 Panamanians live in the United States in the early years of the twenty-first century.

*Above:* **The Palace of Fine Arts in San Francisco was built for the Panama-Pacific International Exposition, held in 1915. The exposition commemorated the completion of the Panama Canal and also the sighting of the Pacific Ocean by Vasco Núñez de Balboa.**

### FAMOUS PANAMANIANS

**Famous Panamanians in the United States include Mariano Rivera (1969– ) and Rolando Blackman (1959– ). Rivera became a pitcher for the New York Yankees in 1995 and continues to live and work in New York today. Although Rolando Blackman is now retired from professional basketball, he played for a total of thirteen years in the National Basketball Association (NBA).**

# Canada-Panama Relations

Although diplomatic relations between Panama and Canada officially began in 1961, Canada did not establish an embassy on the isthmus until 1995. The Canadian embassy was established because of increased Canadian investment in Panama and the growing number of shared political interests between the two countries. In the early twenty-first century, relations between the two nations are mainly trade-related, and David Adam is the Canadian ambassador to Panama.

Leaders of both countries have met in recent years to build stronger political friendships and trade relations. In June 2000, Panamanian first vice president Arturo Vallarino paid an official visit to Canada, where he traveled to Ottawa, Montreal, and Québec City. That same year, Panamanian second vice president Kaiser Bazan, together with leaders of other Central American countries, met with Canadian prime minister Jean Chrétien at the Canada-Central America Summit, held in Guatemala City.

**INDIGENOUS HELP**

In 2001, Québec City hosted the Third Summit of the Americas. Leaders of the involved countries resolved to further their efforts in improving the welfare of the indigenous people of the Americas, who number approximately 50 million. Indigenous people are usually economically disadvantaged, especially those living in remote areas, because they have little access to education or training.

*Left:* Marie Cecile Leanne arrived in Panama City, Panama, on May 15, 2003. Leanne was the Canadian contestant in the Miss Universe 2003 beauty pageant, which was held in Panama.

In April 2001, Panamanian president Mireya Moscoso attended the Third Summit of the Americas, held in Québec City. Panamanian industry and commerce minister Joaquín Jacome and Panamanian foreign affairs vice-minister Nivia Rossana Castrellón visited Ottawa, Canada, in March 2003.

Canadian investment in Panama soared in the 1990s when Canadian mining firms took serious interest in exploiting Panamanian resources. Canadian mining operations, however, began to encroach on and destroy Amerindian territories and drew much resistance from the isthmus's indigenous peoples. The focus of Canadian investments in Panama has since shifted to the production of hydroelectricity by the firm Hydro Québec.

In 2002, trade between Panama and Canada amounted to a total of CAN $49 million, with Panama doing more purchasing than Canada. Panama sold CAN $12.2 million worth of goods, including aluminum, bananas, coffee, and seafood, to Canada. In turn, Panama bought CAN $36.8 million worth of Canadian goods, including iron and steel rails, pharmaceuticals, lentils, pork, cigarettes, and paper products.

*Above:* Canada is one of the countries to which Panama exports bananas. Most of Panama's bananas are grown in the Chiriquí province, located in the western part of the country.

## Canadian Assistance to Panama

Panama receives some financial and development aid from Canada. The Canadian International Development Agency (CIDA), which supports international organizations, such as the United Nations Development Program, the United Nations Children's Fund (UNICEF), and the Inter-American Development Bank, helps Panama in some ways. An example is the U.S. $25-million Regional Electrical Energy Program in the Central American Isthmus Countries (PREEICA), eleven percent of which Panama received to aid its energy distribution. In Panama, the Canadian embassy helps manage the Canada Fund for Local Initiatives on behalf of CIDA. In allocating the resources of the Canada Fund, the embassy pays special attention to Panamanians living in extreme poverty, especially women and children. From 2000 to 2001, the Canada Fund reserved up to CAN $300,000 for Panama. CIDA also offers financial support to Canadian businesses, institutions, and nongovernmental organizations (NGOs) that are engaged in projects that advance development in Panama. From 2000 to 2001, Canada pledged a total of nearly CAN $2 million to aid Panama in its development.

**PREEICA**

CIDA financed the PREEICA project, which was carried out from 1997 to 2004. Apart from Panama, the other countries helped by the project are Costa Rica, El Salvador, Guatemala, Honduras, and Nicaragua. One of the project's aims was to ensure the reliable supply and distribution of electricity in these countries.

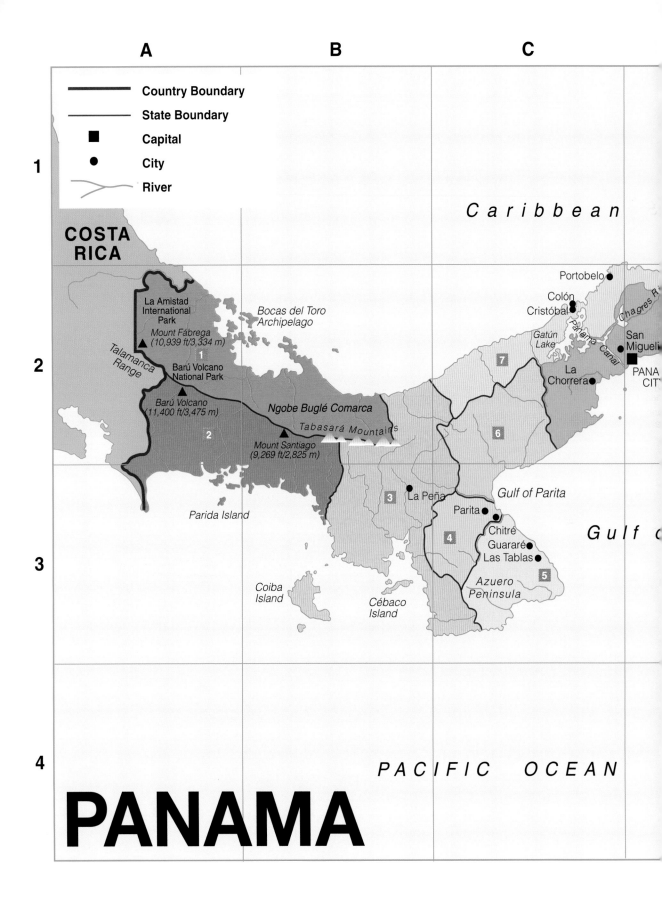

**A**   **B**   **C**

1

—— Country Boundary

—— State Boundary

■ Capital

● City

〜 River

*Caribbean*

COSTA
RICA

Portobelo ●

Colón ●
Cristóbal ●

*Chagres R*

2

La Amistad
International
Park

*Bocas del Toro
Archipelago*

▲ Mount Fábrega
*(10,939 ft/3,334 m)*

**1**

Talamanca
Range

Barú Volcano
National Park

▲
*Barú Volcano
(11,400 ft/3,475 m)*

**2**

*Ngobe Buglé Comarca*

*Tabasará Mountains*

▲ *Mount Santiago
(9,269 ft/2,825 m)*

*Gatún
Lake*

■ PANA
CIT

**7**

San
Migueli ■

La
Chorrera ●

**6**

*Parida Island*

**3** ● La Peña

*Gulf of Parita*

Parita ●

*Gulf o*

3

*Coiba
Island*

*Cébaco
Island*

**4**

Chitré ●
Guararé ●
Las Tablas ●

*Azuero
Peninsula*

**5**

4

*PACIFIC   OCEAN*

# PANAMA

**D**      **E**

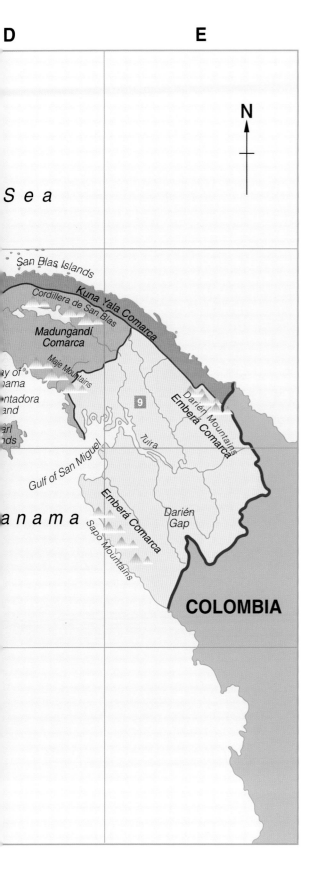

*Sea*

N

San Blas Islands

Kuna Yala Comarca

Cordillera de San Blas

Madungandí
Comarca

Majé Mountains

ay of
ama

ntadora
and

arl
ds

Darién Mountains

Emberá Comarca

Tuira

Gulf of San Miguel

a n a m a

Emberá Comarca

Sapo Mountains

Darién
Gap

9

**COLOMBIA**

**PROVINCES**

1. **Bocas del Toro**

2. **Chiriquí**

3. **Veraguas**

4. **Herrera**

5. **Los Santos**

6. **Coclé**

7. **Colón**

8. **Panama**

9. **Darién**

**Azuero Peninsula B3–C3**

**Barú Volcano A2**
**Barú Volcano National**
**Park A2**
**Bay of Panama C2–D2**
**Bocas del Toro**
**Archipelago A2–B2**

**Caribbean Sea A1–E2**
**Cébaco Island B3**
**Chagres River C2–D2**
**Chitré C3**
**Coiba Island B3**
**Colombia E2–E4**
**Colón (city) C2**
**Contadora Island D2**
**Cordillera de San Blas**
**D2–E2**
**Costa Rica A1–A3**
**Cristóbal (city) C2**

**Darién Gap E3**
**Darién Mountains E2–E3**

**Emberá-Wounaan**
**Comarca E2–E3**

**Gatún Lake C2**
**Guararé (city) C3**
**Gulf of Panama C3–D3**
**Gulf of Parita C2–C3**
**Gulf of San Miguel**
**D3–E2**

**Kuna Yala Comarca**
**D2–E2**

**La Amistad International**
**Park A2**
**La Chorrera (city) C2**
**La Peña (city) B3**
**Las Tablas (city) C3**

**Madungandí Comarca**
**D2–E2**
**Majé Mountains D2**
**Mount Fábrega A2**
**Mount Santiago B2**

**Ngobe Buglé Comarca**
**A2–B3**

**Pacific Ocean A2–E4**
**Panama Canal C2**
**Panama City C2–D2**
**Parida Island A3**
**Parita (city) C3**
**Pearl Islands D2–D3**
**Portobelo (city) C2**

**San Blas Islands D2**
**San Miguelito (city) C2**
**Sapo Mountains D3–E3**

**Tabasará Mountains**
**B2–C2**
**Talamanca Range A2**
**Tuira River E2–E3**

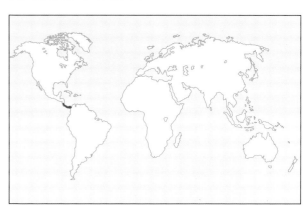

87

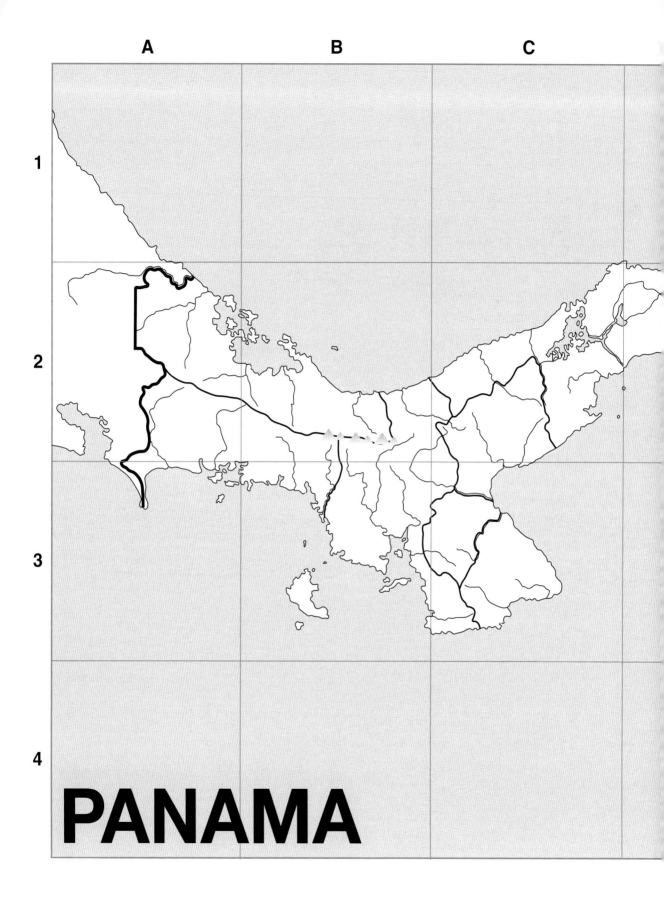

A B C

1

2

3

4

# PANAMA

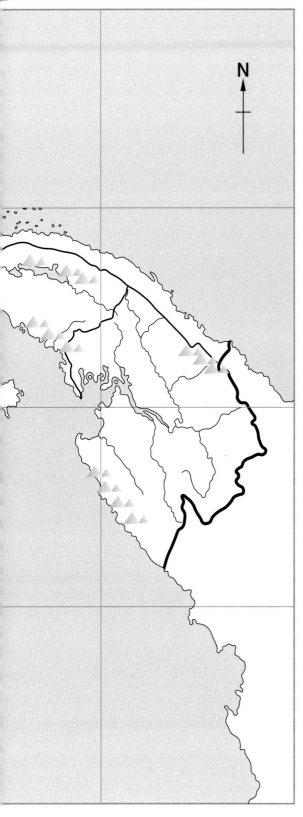

N

# How Is Your Geography?

Learning to identify the main geographical areas and points of a country can be challenging. Although it may seem difficult at first to memorize the locations and spellings of major cities or the names of mountain ranges, rivers, deserts, lakes, and other prominent physical features, the end result of this effort can be very rewarding. Places you previously did not know existed will suddenly come to life when referred to in world news, whether in newspapers, television reports, other books and reference sources, or on the Internet. This knowledge will make you feel a bit closer to the rest of the world, with its fascinating variety of cultures and physical geography.

This map can be duplicated for use in a classroom. (PLEASE DO NOT WRITE IN THIS BOOK!) Students can then fill in any requested information on their individual map copies. The student can also make a copy of the map and use it as a study tool to practice identifying place names and geographical features on his or her own.

# Panama at a Glance

**Offical Name**    Republic of Panama

**Capital**      Panama City

**Official Language**  Spanish

**Population**     3,120,000 (2004 estimate)

**Ethnic Groups**   Mestizo (70 percent), West Indian (14 percent), Caucasian (10 percent), Amerindian (6 percent).

**Land Area**     30,185 square miles (78,200 square kilometers)

**Provinces**     Bocas del Toro, Chiriquí, Coclé, Colón, Darién, Herrera, Los Santos, Panama, Veraguas

**Indigenous Territories**  Kuna Yala, Emberá, Madungandí, Ngobe Buglé

**Highest Point**   Barú Volcano 11,400 feet (3,475 m)

**Major Rivers**    Chagres, Tuira

**Famous Leaders**  Manuel Amador Guerrero (1833–1909)

          Omar Torrijos Herrera (1929–1981)

          Manuel Antonio Noriega Morena (1938– )

          Mireya Elisa Moscoso de Gruber (1946– )

**Major Cities**    Panama City, Cólon, David, Santiago

**Main Religion**   Roman Catholicism (85 percent)

**Major Exports**   Bananas, seafood, sugar, coffee, clothing

**Major Imports**   Crude oil, chemicals, food, consumer goods

**Major Trade Partners**  United States, Sweden, Nicaragua, Ecuador, Costa Rica, Venezuela, Japan

**Currency**     Balboa (PAB 1 = U.S. $1 as of 2003)

          Note: U.S. dollars are legal tender in Panama.

*Opposite:* **A Kuna Amerindian woman sits in front of her hanging display of mola stitchwork while she waits for customers.**

# Glossary

## Spanish Vocabulary

*arroz con guando* (ah-ROHS con GUAN-doh): a Panamanian side dish made from cooking rice and beans in coconut milk.

*audiencia* (aw-dee-EN-see-ah): a territory that has rights similar to those of a state government in a federation.

*ceviche* (seh-VEE-sheh): a popular Panamanian appetizer made of raw fish soaked in a marinade of lemon or lime juice, chopped onions, salt, pepper, and olive oil that is served chilled and with crackers on the side.

*chichas* (CHEE-chas): a refreshing drink made by mixing fruit juices with water and sugar and served chilled or topped with ice.

*chicheme* (shi-SHE-mei): a drink made by cooking cornmeal with water, sugar, and cinnamon.

*cocadas* (koh-KAH-dahs): a type of coconut-flavored candy.

*comarca* (kow-MAHR-kah): a territory specifically reserved for one or more indigenous groups.

*ferias* (FEH-ree-ahs): trade fairs.

*fufu* (FOO-FOO): a Panamanian seafood dish made from cooking pieces of plantains, yams, and fried fish in coconut milk.

*hojaldras* (ou-HAHL-drahs): a flat piece of fried dough, usually served with sugar, that is eaten at breakfast or as a snack.

*Kuna* (KOO-nah): one of the three main Amerindian groups in Panama.

*mola* (MOU-lah): a form of stitchwork produced by sewing together many layers of cloth using the reverse appliqué technique.

*pollera* (pou-YEH-rah): the national dress of Panama.

*quequis* (KEH-kihs): cookies made from flour, coconut, honey, and ginger spices.

*raspado* (rahs-PAH-dou): a Panamanian dessert consisting of a cone of crushed ice topped with a variety of syrups and sweetened, condensed milk.

*sancocho* (sahn-KOH-shoh): a hearty chicken-and-vegetable soup that is a classic Panamanian dish.

*tamale* (tah-MAHL): a Panamanian dish consisting of cooked pockets of cornmeal dough stuffed with meat and vegetables and wrapped in banana leaves.

*Tamborito* (TAHM-boh-REE-toh): Panama's national dance; the word literally means "little drum."

## English Vocabulary

**abstaining:** voluntarily avoiding an object or action; not voting for or against a proposal when a vote is held.

**amassing:** gathering.

**Amerindian:** American Indian; referring to the various tribes of native Indians from the American continents.

**anthropologists:** experts in the science of human origins, who study physical and cultural development, biological characteristics, and the social customs and beliefs of humans.

**archaeological:** relating to the study of material remains (fossil relics, artifacts, and monuments) of past human life and activities.

**autonomy:** the right or ability of self-government.

**beheaded:** having one's head cut off; decapitated.

**broiled:** cooked using direct heat.

**cacao:** the dried seeds of a South American tree that are used in making cocoa and chocolate.

**cassava:** a type of root vegetable, also known as tapioca, manioc, or yucca.

**castanets:** a small instrument consisting of two round shells of wood that are held in the palm of the hand and clicked together to make sounds.

**centennial:** marking the completion of a period of 100 years.

**coalition:** a union of different groups or parties for joint action.

**disarray:** disorder and confusion.

**doctrines:** teachings; often ideas taught as principles of a religion.

**ecotourism:** tourism that focuses on and respects the beauty and spectacle of a country's natural environment.

**en route:** on or along the way.

**encroach:** to make gradual inroads into or to trespass stealthily upon the property of another.

**federation:** a type of government consisting of a central government under which individual governments that control states are surbordinate.

**hub:** a center of activity, authority, and commerce.

**illustrious:** highly distinguished.

**isthmus:** a narrow strip of land that is bordered on both sides by water and connects two larger bodies of land.

**inlet:** an indentation in a shoreline.

**junta:** a small group ruling a country, usually after a revolution.

**legacy:** something handed down from an ancestor.

**maritime:** relating to shipping or navigating the sea.

**montane:** the belt of vegetation found on the lower parts of a mountain.

**pidgin:** a simplified language made up of two or more languages that is used for communication between speakers whose native languages are different.

**plantain:** a starchy fruit that resembles a green banana but requires cooking before being eaten and tastes like potato.

**plumage:** the entire feathery covering of a bird.

**pre-Columbian:** relating to the Americas before the arrival of Christopher Columbus.

**proficient:** fully competent or expert in a given subject.

**sanitation:** the disposal of sewage and solid waste.

**savannas:** plains characterized by coarse grasses and scattered tree growth.

**thatched:** having a covering made from leaves, straw, or similar materials.

**trawlers:** vessels that drag nets to catch fish.

**viceroyalty:** a country or province ruled by a viceroy, who is a person appointed as the deputy of a king or queen.

**yam:** a type of root vegetable, also known as a sweet potato.

# More Books to Read

*Into Wild Panama.*  Elaine Pascoe (Blackbirch Marketing)

*It's Panama's Canal!*  Patricia Maloney Markun (Linnet Books)

*Panama. Let's Discover Central America* series.  Charles J. Shields and James D. Henderson (Mason Crest)

*Panama. Major World Nations* series.  Tricia Haynes (Chelsea House)

*Panama. True Book* series.  Dana Meachen Rau (Scholastic Library)

*The Panama Canal. Great Building Feats* series.  Lesley A. Dutemple (Lerner Publications)

*Panama Canal in American History. In American History* series.  Ann Graham Gaines (Enslow Publishing)

*Ruben Blades. Hispanics of Achievement* series.  Betty A. Marton (Chelsea House)

*Story in the Stone: The Formation of a Tropical Land Bridge.*  Tom Gidwitz (Raintree/ Steck-Vaughn)

# Videos

*Modern Marvels: Panama Canal.* (A&E Home Video)

*Nova: A Man, A Plan, A Canal, Panama.* (WGBH Boston)

*Secrets of War: Bold Strikes — The Invasion of Panama.* (Image Entertainment)

# Web Sites

www.cia.gov/cia/publications/factbook/print/pm.html

www.orbi.net/pancanal/pcc.htm

www.panamaaudubon.org

www.trainweb.org/panama/

Due to the dynamic nature of the Internet, some web sites stay current longer than others. To find additional web sites, use a reliable search engine with one or more of the following keywords to help you locate information about Panama. Keywords: *Azuero Peninsula, Darién Jungle, Manuel Noriega, Panama Canal, Pearl Islands.*

# Index